Anonymous

Documents Relating to the Formation of the Chicago and North Western Railway Company

Anonymous

Documents Relating to the Formation of the Chicago and North Western Railway Company

ISBN/EAN: 9783744724920

Printed in Europe, USA, Canada, Australia, Japan

Cover: Foto ©ninafisch / pixelio.de

More available books at **www.hansebooks.com**

DOCUMENTS

RELATING TO

THE FORMATION

OF THE

CHICAGO AND NORTH WESTERN

RAILWAY COMPANY.

New-York:

JOHN W. AMERMAN, PRINTER
No. 47 Cedar Street.

1860.

DOCUMENTS.

A·N ACT

TO AUTHORIZE THE SALE OF THE CHICAGO, ST. PAUL AND FOND DU LAC RAIL-ROAD, AND TO ENABLE THE PURCHASERS THEREOF TO FORM AS A CORPORATION.

[Passed February 19, 1859.]

SECTION 1. *Be it enacted by the People of the State of Illinois, represented in the General Assembly,* That if any mortgage or deed of trust, heretofore or hereafter executed by the Chicago, St. Paul and Fond du Lac Rail-Road Company, a corporation existing under and by virtue of the laws of this State, shall be foreclosed either by bill in chancery or by publication of notice in the manner prescribed in such mortgage or deed of trust, and there shall be a sale of said Chicago, St. Paul and Fond du Lac Rail-Road, or any part of it, on or by virtue of any trust deed, or on foreclosure of any mortgage thereupon, the party or parties acquiring title under any such sale, and their associates, successors or assigns, shall have and acquire thereby, and shall exercise and enjoy thereafter, all and the same rights, privileges, grants, franchises, immunities and advantages in and by said mortgage or trust deed enumerated and conveyed which belonged to and were enjoyed by the said Chicago, St. Paul and Fond du Lac Rail-Road Company, as fully and absolutely in all respects as the Chicago, St. Paul and Fond du Lac Rail-Road Company, its corporators, shareholders, officers and agents might or could have done theretofore had not such sale or foreclosure taken place. Such purchaser or purchasers, their associates, successors or assigns, may proceed to organize anew and elect directors, distribute and dispose of stock, take the same or another name, and may conduct their business generally under and in the manner provided in the charter and rights of said Chicago, St. Paul and Fond du Lac Rail-Road Company, under and by virtue of its consolidations with other rail-road companies, and generally to do and perform all things said Chicago, St.

Paul and Fond du Lac Rail-Road Company might do under and by virtue of any laws of this or any other State through which the line of said company's road runs or is located, or under the chartered privileges or rights acquired by charters of and consolidations with other rail-road companies in such other States, with such variations in manner and form of organization as their altered circumstances and better conveniences may seem to require.

SEC. 2. Said new corporation, when so organized, shall have full power to mortgage, lease or pledge their said road, or any portion of the same, and any other estate, real, personal or mixed, of which they may be seised at the time of or which they may acquire after the execution of such mortgage, deed of trust or other instrument in writing to secure any bonds or indebtedness or evidence of indebtedness of said corporation so created as aforesaid, or to pay for the whole or any part of the purchase money or cost of said road at the sale thereof to the purchasers thereof, their associates, successors or assigns, or to pay, fund or liquidate any existing liabilities or indebtedness of said Chicago, St. Paul and Fond du Lac Rail-Road Company, which said purchasers, their associates, successors or assigns, may agree or elect to assume and provide for.

SEC. 3. Said corporation is hereby authorized and fully empowered, in its corporate capacity, to borrow any sum or sums of money from any person or persons, corporation or body politic of any kind, and for any rate of interest which may be agreed upon by and between said company and the party to whom such money may be obtained, and to make, execute and deliver, in or out of this State, all necessary writings, notes, bonds, bills, mortgages, deeds of trust and all other papers or securities in amount or kind as may be deemed expedient by said corporation in consideration of any such loan, or in discharge of any liability they may incur in the purchase, construction, repair, equipment or operation of said road, or in any of the transactions of said company. And said company is hereby authorized, in its corporate capacity, to make, execute, issue and deliver its bonds or obligations in such amounts as the directors of said company shall deem for the best interests of said company, and the directors of said company shall prescribe the sum or sums for which each of said bonds shall be issued, and the time or times and place or places when and where the principal and interest of the same shall be payable, the rate of interest which said bonds shall bear, and the manner and form in which the same, and the interest coupons annexed to the same, shall be executed; and to secure the payment of any and all of said bonds, the said company is hereby authorized and empowered, in its corporate capacity, to make, execute and deliver a mortgage or mortgages, or deed or deeds of trust upon the whole or any part of said rail-road, constructed or not constructed, and authorized to be purchased by this act, and upon any other and all of its estate, real, personal or mixed, in possession or expectancy; and the said company is hereby authorized and empowered, in and by such mortgage or deed of trust, to confer upon the mortgagee or trustee full and ample power to enter into and upon and take possession of, have, use and enjoy, or sell or dispose of the whole or any part of said rail-road or estate, real, personal or mixed, together with the functions pertaining to said rail-road, and all other corporate and other franchises, rights and privileges of the said rail-road company, to take up and remove any of the track or fixtures belonging to said rail-road; and the directors of said company shall prescribe all matters relating to the form and terms of said mortgage or deeds of trust, and the manner and mode for the execution of the same, and may provide for the payment of the principal and interest secured to be paid by such bonds, either by the creation of a sinking fund out of the earnings of said rail-road company, or in any other manner that they may deem best for the interest of said company; and said company may, by its agents in or out of the State, sell, dispose of, or hypothecate such bonds when so issued as aforesaid, at par or at any other price greater or less than par, and for such sum or sums as they may think proper.

Sec. 4. And it may be lawful for the meetings of stockholders, directors or officers of said company, when so organized, to be held within or without this State, at such time and place or places as the by-laws of said company or the board of directors may from time appoint.

Sec. 5. This act shall be a public act and shall be in force from and after its passage.

Wm. R. Morrison,
Speaker of the House of Representatives.

John Wood,
Speaker of the Senate.

Approved February 19, 1859.

Wm. H. Bissell.

UNITED STATES OF AMERICA, }
    State of Illinois, } ss.

I, O. M. Hatch, Secretary of State of the State of Illinois,
do hereby certify the foregoing to be a true and
correct copy of an enrolled law now on file in my
[L. S.]   office. In witness whereof, I have hereunto set my
hand, and caused the great seal of State to be affixed. Done at Springfield, this 21st day of February, 1859.

O. M. HATCH, *Secretary.*

AN ACT

TO FACILITATE AND AUTHENTICATE THE FORMATION OF A CORPO-
RATION BY THE PURCHASERS OF THE CHICAGO, ST. PAUL AND
FOND DU LAC RAIL-ROAD COMPANY :

[Passed March 14, 1859.]

*The People of the State of Wisconsin, represented in Senate
and Assembly, do enact as follows :*

SECTION 1. In case the rail-road of the Chicago, St. Paul
and Fond du Lac Rail-Road Company, or any part of the
said rail-road lying within this State, shall. be sold by virtue
of any mortgage or mortgages, deed or deeds of trust, either
by foreclosure or other proceedings in law or equity, or by
advertisement, in pursuance of a power or authority in any
such mortgage or deed of trust contained, the purchaser or
purchasers in any such case, his or their associates, successors or assigns, if desiring to form a corporation under or by
virtue of the laws of this State, or of the States of Illinois or
Michigan, or of any or all of said States, may file in the
office of the Secretary of State of this State a certificate,
specifying the name of the said corporation, the number of
the directors, and the names of the directors for the first
year, as designated in the said certificate, or as elected by
the said purchaser or purchasers, their successors or assigns ;
which certificate shall be signed by the said purchaser or
purchasers, or the survivor of them, or their or his successors
or assigns ; and upon the filing of any such certificate, the
persons who shall have signed the same shall be a body

politic and corporate by the name stated in such certificate; and the said corporation shall possess all the privileges, powers, authorities and capacities acquired by the said purchaser or purchasers, or possessed by the Chicago, St. Paul and Fond du Lac Rail-Road Company, by virtue of any law of this State, or of the States of Illinois or Michigan; and shall likewise have power, by the vote of a majority in interest of the stockholders of the said corporation, and by instruments in writing, to assume any debts or liabilities of the said Chicago, St. Paul and Fond du Lac Rail-Road Company, and secure the same in the same manner as the said corporation might secure any debt contracted for the completion of said road, or for any other purpose; and shall also have power to create and issue a special stock to represent its lands and bonds; which stock shall be subject to assessments and entitled to dividends only to such extent and upon such conditions as shall be fixed by the act or agreement of the corporation creating the said stock, and not otherwise, but may be voted on the same as other stock.

SEC. 2. This act shall take effect and be in force from and after its passage.

WM. P. LYON,
Speaker of the Assembly.

E. D. CAMPBELL,
Lieutenant Governor and
President of the Senate.

Approved March 14th, 1859.

ALEX. W. RANDALL.

STATE OF WISCONSIN, }
  Secretary's Office, } ss.

The Secretary of State of the State of Wisconsin does hereby certify that the foregoing act has been compared with the original enrolled act filed in this office, and that the same is a true and correct copy thereof, and of the whole of such original.

In witness whereof, I have hereunto set my hand, and affixed the great seal of the State, at the capitol in [L. S.] Madison, this 21st day of June, A. D. 1859.

J. D. RUGGLES,
Ass't Secretary of State.

GENERAL PLAN OF RE-ORGANIZATION.

WHEREAS the CHICAGO, ST. PAUL AND FOND DU LAC RAIL-ROAD COMPANY has become embarrassed and unable to complete its road, or pay the interest on its bonds, secured by its first and second mortgages :

AND WHEREAS it is represented that the Trustees, under the said mortgages, are about to sell the said road and its appurtenances, whereby the interests of the unsecured creditors and stockholders would be divested and destroyed :

AND WHEREAS an amicable and harmonious adjustment of all interests involved in the enterprise, which, while it shall protect existing priorities of the bondholders, shall, at the same time, preserve other interests from absolute extinction, and secure general co-operation in the completion of the road, and in promoting its business, is believed to be for the substantial and ultimate advantage of all parties :

AND WHEREAS a meeting of all the various classes of parties in interest, whether as first or second mortgage bondholders, creditors or stockholders, was held at the Office of the Company in the City of New-York, on the 22d of February, 1859, and after mature consideration and full discussion, a plan for the purpose of carrying out the aforesaid objects was unanimously adopted, which said plan is substantially as follows :

THE PLAN.

It is proposed that the rail-road, and all the property connected therewith, shall be bought by persons who shall be agents of the subscribing bondholders for such purchase, and that a corporation or corporations shall be organized under the laws of Wisconsin, Illinois and Michigan, or under the laws of some of these States, and the stock created and securities made, of the said corporation or corporations, shall be distributed in the manner and on the conditions hereinafter expressed.

1st. Bonds shall be created to the amount of four millions five hundred thousand dollars, in sums not less than one hundred dollars, nor exceeding one thousand dollars each ; three millions five hundred thousand dollars of which shall be for substitution for the present first mortgage bonds and coupons, and one million of dollars of which shall be for the completion of the road, and the discharge of special liens upon the equipment, and, as far as may be, on the depot grounds, and for other necessary purposes in carrying out the objects herein expressed; and at least $600,000 of which shall be inviolably appropriated and applied to the said work of construction. And the said provision of one million of dollars and the aggregate amount of the bonds, may be enlarged by an amount not exceeding one hundred thousand dollars, in case such an increase shall prove necessary for the said work of construction. The three millions five hundred thousand dollars shall be payable in New-York at twenty-five years from the first of August, 1860, with interest from the first of August, 1860; the one million dollars shall be payable at such times as shall hereafter be fixed, with interest from the first of August, 1859. The interest shall be seven per cent., payable semi-annually, in New-York. The one million dollars shall be entitled to priority under the same mortgage, and to the benefit of a sinking fund to be therein provided. The whole of the said bonds shall be secured by a first mortgage upon the franchises of the corporation, the rail-road from Chicago to a point twenty miles north of Fond du Lac, or if deemed advisable, to Oshkosh, and its equipment and appurtenances, whether now possessed or hereafter acquired.

2d. Bonds shall also be created to the amount of two millions of dollars, payable in thirty years from November 1st, 1860, with interest at six per cent. from that date, to be secured by a second mortgage on the road and property, before mentioned.

3d. Stock shall be created to an amount adequate to the requirements hereinafter expressed.

4th. A special stock or optional stock, of two classes, to be denominated Bond Stock and Land Stock, to an amount required by the provisions hereinafter contained, shall be created as soon after this agreement shall have gone into operation as the same can be lawfully and conveniently created; which said stock shall be inseparably attached to the bonds and land certificates, and shall entitle the holder thereof to vote at all meetings equally with other stock; but shall not entitle the holder to dividends, or be subject to assessment.

I. First Mortgage Bondholders.

Holders of the present first mortgage bonds of the company acceding to this plan and performing all its conditions, shall be entitled to its benefits, viz.:

1st. They shall subscribe at par for bonds (parcel of the

one million included in the first mortgage to be made) to an amount equal to ten per cent. on the par value of the bonds held by them respectively, and pay the said subscription at the times and in the manner to be provided in pursuance hereof.

2d. They shall surrender or assign, as they may be required, to persons designated for the purpose, the bonds so held by them and the coupons issued therewith and remaining unpaid.

3. They shall thereupon become entitled to new bonds, (parcel of the three millions five hundred thousand dollars, included in the first mortgage,) equal in par value to the par value of the bonds and coupons so surrendered or assigned, except as to fractional amounts less than the amount of a bond issued, for which scrip certificates may be given, not bearing interest until aggregated and converted into bonds.

4th. They shall also become entitled to an amount of the optional bond stock, whenever the same shall have been created, equal to fifty per cent. on the par value of the bonds subscribed for, or converted as aforesaid.

II. Second Mortgage or Land Grant Bondholders.

Holders of the present second mortgage or land grant bonds, acceding to this plan and performing all its conditions, shall become entitled to its benefits, viz.:

1st. They shall subscribe at par for bonds (parcel of the one million included in the first mortgage to be made) to an amount equal to ten per cent. on the par value of the bonds held by them respectively, and pay the said subscriptions at the times and in the manner to be provided in pursuance hereof.

2d. They shall surrender or assign, as they may be required, to persons designated for the purpose, the bonds so held by them and the coupons issued therewith and remaining unpaid.

3d. They shall thereupon become entitled to new bonds, (parcel of the two millions of dollars,) secured by the second mortgage to be made as herein provided, to the extent of sixty-six and two-thirds per cent. upon the par value of the bonds so surrendered or assigned, except as to fractional amounts less than the amount of a bond issued, for which scrip certificates may be given, not bearing interest until aggregated and converted into bonds.

4th. They shall also become entitled, in proportion to the bonds and coupons surrendered or assigned by them respectively, to all the rights included in the present land grant mortgage in the one hundred and fifty-three thousand six hundred acres of land, more or less, to accrue on the completion of the road to a point twenty miles north of Fond du Lac, and shall receive as evidence thereof, land stock certificates, not exceeding the nominal amount of $1,800,000, containing provisions making the same convertible into said lands, and upon which the holders of said stock may vote until so converted, but the same shall not be assessable or entitled to dividends.

5th. They shall also be entitled to an amount of optional bond stock, whenever the same shall have been created, equal to fifty per cent. of the par value of the bonds converted as aforesaid, not exceeding two millions of dollars in amount.

III. General or Unsecured Creditors.

The general or unsecured creditors, acceding to this plan and performing all its conditions, may be admitted to its benefits, viz.:

1st. They shall surrender or assign, as may be required, to persons designated for the purpose, their debts and all the evidences thereof.

2d. They shall be entitled to receive stock to the amount of seventy-five per cent. of the amount found to be payable to them respectively, including interest to the day of the date hereof; but in all cases where a debt shall have been secured or partially secured by collaterals, the rule for the adjustment shall be prescribed by the persons purchasing and acting as agents of subscribing bondholders, upon principles which they shall deem equitable, and the amount to be allowed, and the terms of said allowance, shall be finally determined by them.

IV. Stockholders.

Shareholders acceding to this plan and performing all its conditions may be admitted to its benefits as follows:

1st. They shall surrender or assign, as they may be required, to persons designated for the purpose, the stock which they respectively hold.

2d. They shall be entitled to receive an amount of the stock of the new corporation to be created, equal to sixty per cent. of the par value of the stock now held by them respectively; but this provision shall only apply to *bona fid* holders of stock.

General Provisions.

1st. The times for the performance of the conditions of this plan by the several classes of first and second mortgage bond-holders, creditors and stockholders shall be fixed by the persons purchasing and acting as agents of subscribing bond-holders as above mentioned, or by the corporation or corporations which may be formed in pursuance hereof. On default to perform all the conditions of this agreement, all rights of the person so in default, by virtue of this agreement, shall cease.

2d. All questions in respect to the construction or effect of any provision of this plan shall be submitted to the purchasers or purchaser herein mentioned, and their decision shall be final and conclusive; and they are hereby vested with full power to carry out the provisions of this plan; and in any case which is unprovided for by this plan, to supply the defect, and generally to do all acts and things necessary to carry out the objects of this plan.

3d. All parties must accede to this plan within sixty days from March 1st, 1859, or they will not afterwards become entitled to its benefits, unless by the written consent of the said purchasers or purchaser, except foreign bondholders, creditors and stockholders, for whom they shall fix what they may deem to be a further reasonable time.

AGREEMENT

OF FIRST MORTGAGE BONDHOLDERS SUBSCRIBING HERETO.

Now, therefore, each of the persons, being a holder of the aforesaid first mortgage bonds and subscribing this instrument, in consideration of the mutual undertakings herein contained, hereby agrees to and with each and all the other persons, being also holders of the said bonds and subscribing this instrument, that he, the person so agreeing, accepts of, and consents to, the terms and conditions applying to the first mortgage bonds of the said Chicago, St. Paul and Fond du Lac Rail-Road Company, and the coupons thereunto belonging, expressed in the aforesaid plan, for and with respect to the bonds and coupons belonging thereto, held by the said person so agreeing, being the number of said bonds by the said person set opposite his name affixed hereto; and that he, the person so agreeing, will subscribe for bonds hereafter to be made by the corporation or corporations, to be formed by the purchaser or purchasers, the survivor of them, or his or their assigns, being parcel of the bonds amounting in the aggregate to one million of dollars, which are to be secured by the first mortgage to be made by said corporation or corporations, with the priorities in the said plan mentioned, to the extent of ten per cent. on the par value of the present bonds by him set opposite his name affixed hereto; and will pay the amount of the said subscription to the said corporation or corporations to be formed as aforesaid, or to the person or persons who may be designated by the said corporation or corporations for the said purpose, in such instalments, and at such times and places as the said corporation or corporations may prescribe; and will deliver and assign the bonds of the present mortgage, by him hereto subscribed, to the number by him set opposite to his name affixed hereunto, with the coupons belonging thereto, (being all the coupons issued therewith and remaining unpaid,) to such person or persons as may be designated for that purpose by the purchasers or purchaser, or the survivor or assigns of the said purchasers or purchaser, and at such times and places as may be by them appointed, and will accept in exchange therefor an amount equal to the par of the said bonds and coupons, in the bonds to be secured by the first mortgage to be made by the corporation or corporations to be hereafter created, and being parcel of the three and a half millions in the aforesaid plan mentioned.

And for the considerations aforesaid, each of the said persons so subscribing does hereby irrevocably constitute and appoint SAMUEL J. TILDEN and O. D. ASHLEY, and either of them, to be his agents and attorneys in fact, with authority in his name and stead to attend any sale or sales of the Chicago, St. Paul and Fond du Lac Rail-Road, or of any part of said rail-road, or of the property appertaining thereto, whenever and wherever the same may be offered for sale, under or by virtue of the said first mortgage given to secure the payment of the bonds held by the said subscriber in common with other bonds; and in their or his discretion to bid for and purchase in their names, or the name of either of them, or such other name as they may deem best, and by themselves or their agents and attorneys, at the said sale or sales, the said Chicago, St. Paul and Fond du Lac Rail-Road, together with its appurtenances, and all and singular, the property, rights and things of every nature embraced in the said first mortgage of the said Chicago, St. Paul and Fond du Lac Rail-Road Company, bearing date on the first day of August, A. D. 1855, or any part of the said rail-road or property; *provided always*, and this authority is upon the express condition that the said subscriber shall be interested in the said bid or bids, and purchase or purchases, in the same proportion which the bonds held by him and set opposite to his signature affixed hereto, with the coupons belonging thereto, shall bear to the whole number of bonds secured by the said first mortgage, with the coupons belonging thereto, and that the said subscriber shall not be made, nor in any way construed or held to become liable for the said bid or bids, or the said purchase or purchases, to any extent exceeding the amount of the bonds set opposite his name affixed hereto, and the coupons representing the accrued interest thereon up to February first, 1859.

And it is hereby mutually agreed, that each person subscribing hereto and holding the bonds so subscribed, may become entitled to an interest in the proportion which his bonds bear to the whole number of bonds subscribed, (on furnishing to the said agents in a manner satisfactory to them, and at least thirty days before the time appointed for the said sale, funds to defray the cost of such interest,) in that portion of the purchase or purchases which may be acquired in consequence of any bondholders under the present mortgage not becoming parties hereto; *provided*, that any such right shall be subject to the option of the purchaser or purchasers, to allow any such non-subscribing bondholder subsequently to become a party hereto, on such terms as to the said purchasers or purchaser may seem expedient; and it is further agreed, that in case any of the parties hereto shall decline, or omit to accept, or to comply with this provision, or shall fail to fulfil his obligations under this agreement, the said agents may hold the aforesaid portion of the purchase or purchases for their own account and benefit; and that in all cases, the parties acquiring any such interest, shall be entitled, in all respects, to stand as to the new securities to be issued, in the place of the non-subscribing bondholders, to whose interest under this agreement they may have thus succeeded.

And the said agents and attorneys, or such of them as may become purchasers or purchaser at the sale or sales aforesaid, are hereby declared to possess and are invested with all the legal powers and rights of purchasers or purchasor, as will with respect to any interest which any party hereto may be entitled to acquire in any bid or bids, as with respect to any other interest therein, and shall have full authority to convey all the interests and rights acquired by any such bid or bids, purchase or purchases, to any corporation or corporations which may be formed for the purpose of holding and operating the said rail-road, or any part thereof, with such restrictions, conditions and agreements from the said corporation or corporations, as to the said purchasers or purchaser may seem expedient; and generally to do all acts and things for the formation of the said corporation or corporations, and for investing them when so formed with the rail-road and property acquired by any such purchase or purchases.

And each of the persons subscribing hereto agrees to furnish his quota of the money necessary to defray the expenses and charges which may be incurred in the said sales or in the creation of the said corporation or corporations, or in the full carrying out of the agreements herein contemplated.

And it is further mutually agreed, that this agreement may be enforced as against any party hereto by action brought in the name of any person who may be designated by the said purchasers or purchaser for that purpose, or in the name of the corporation or corporations hereafter to be created, as herein provided, and that in case any party hereto shall fail to comply with all of the conditions and provisions of this agreement, the rights of such party, by virtue thereof, may, at the option of said purchasers or purchaser, or of the said corporation or corporations, be declared forfeited, and thereupon all interests of the said party, under or by virtue of this agreement, shall absolutely cease.

IN WITNESS WHEREOF, we have hereunto set our hands, on the 16th day of March, 1859, and have affixed opposite to our names the number of bonds by us respectively subscribed hereto or to duplicates hereof.

AGREEMENT

OF SECOND MORTGAGE LAND GRANT BONDHOLDERS SUBSCRIBING HERETO.

Now, therefore, each of the persons, being a holder of the aforesaid second mortgage land grant bonds and subscribing this instrument, in consideration of the mutual undertakings herein contained, hereby agrees to and with each and all the other persons, being also holders of the said bonds and subscribing this instrument, that he, the person so agreeing, accepts of, and consents to, the terms and conditions applying to the second mortgage land grant bonds of the said Chicago, St. Paul and Fond Du Lac Rail-Road Company, and the coupons thereunto belonging, expressed in the aforesaid plan, for and with respect to the bonds and coupons belonging thereto, held by the said persons so agreeing, being the number of said bonds by the said person set opposite his name affixed hereto, and that he, the person so agreeing, will subscribe for bonds hereafter to be made by the corporation or corporations, to be formed by the purchaser or purchasers, the survivor of them, or his or their assigns, being parcel of the bonds amounting in the aggregate to one million of dollars, which are to be secured by the first mortgage to be made by said corporation or corporations, with the priorities in the said plan mentioned, to the extent of ten per cent. on the par value of the present bonds by him set opposite his name affixed hereto, and will pay the amount of the said subscription to the said corporation or corporations to be formed as aforesaid, or to the person or persons who may be designated by the said corporation or corporations for the said purpose, in such installments, and at such times and places as the said corporation or corporations may prescribe; and will deliver and assign the bonds of the present second land grant mortgage, by him hereto subscribed, to the number by him set opposite to his name affixed hereunto, with the coupons belonging thereto, (being all the coupons issued therewith and remaining unpaid,) to such person or persons as may be designated for that purpose by the purchasers or purchaser, or the survivor or assigns of the said purchasers or purchaser, and at such times and places as may be by them appointed, and will accept in exchange therefor an amount equal to sixty-six and two-thirds per cent. of the par of the said bonds, in the bonds to be secured by the second mortgage to be made by the corporation or corporations to be hereafter created, and being parcel of the two millions in the aforesaid plan mentioned; and the balance of said bonds, and the coupons by him so as aforesaid delivered and assigned, in the land scrip or stock to be issued by the corporation or corporations hereafter to be created, and being parcel of the one million eight hundred thousand in the aforesaid plan mentioned.

And for the considerations aforesaid, each of the said persons so subscribing does hereby irrevocably constitute and appoint SAMUEL J. TILDEN and O. D. ASHLEY and either of them, to be his agents and attorneys in fact, with authority in his name and stead to attend any sale or sales of the Chicago, St. Paul and Fond du Lac Rail-Road, or of any part of said rail-road, or of the property appertaining thereto, whenever and wherever the same may be offered for sale, under or by virtue of the said second land grant mortgage given to secure the payment of the bonds held by the said subscriber in common with other bonds; and in their or his discretion to bid for and purchase in their names, or the name of either of them, or such other name as they may deem best, and by themselves or their agents and attorneys, at the said sale or sales, the said Chicago, St. Paul and Fond du Lac Rail-Road, together with its appurtenances, and all and singular, the property, rights and things of every nature embraced in the said second land grant mortgage of the said Chicago, St. Paul and Fond du Lac Rail-Road Company, bearing date on the sixth day of April, A. D. 1857, or any part of the said rail-road or property; *provided always*, and this authority is upon the express condition that the said subscriber shall be interested in the said bid or bids, and purchase or purchases, in the same proportion which the bonds held by him and set opposite his signature affixed hereto, with the coupons belonging thereto, shall bear to the whole number of bonds secured by the said second land grant mortgage, with the coupons belonging thereto, and that the said subscriber shall not be made, nor in any way construed or held to become liable for the said bid or bids, or the said purchase or purchases, to any extent exceeding the amount of the bonds set opposite his name affixed hereto, and the coupons representing the accrued interest thereon up to November first, 1860.

And it is hereby mutually agreed, that each person subscribing hereto and holding the bonds so subscribed, may become entitled to an interest in the proportion which his bonds bear to the whole number of bonds subscribed, (on furnishing to the said agents in a manner satisfactory to them, and at least thirty days before the time appointed for the said sale, funds to defray the cost of such interest,) in that portion of the purchase or purchases which may be acquired in consequence of any bondholders under the present second or land grant mortgage not becoming parties hereto; *provided*, that any such right shall be subject to the option of the purchaser or purchasers, to allow any such non-subscribing bondholder subsequently to become a party hereto, on such terms as to the said purchasers or purchaser may deem expedient; and it is further agreed, that in case any of the parties hereto shall decline, or omit to accept, or to comply with

2

this provision, or shall fail to fulfil his obligations under this agreement, the said agents may hold the aforesaid portion of the purchase or purchases for their own account and benefit; and that in all cases, the parties acquiring any such interest, shall be entitled, in all respects, to stand as to the new securities to be issued, in the place of the non-subscribing bondholders, to whose interest under this agreement they may have thus succeeded.

And the said agents and attorneys, or such of them as may become purchasers or purchaser at the sale or sales aforesaid, are hereby declared to possess and are invested with all the legal powers and rights of purchasers or purchaser, as well with respect to any interest which any party hereto may be entitled to acquire in any bid or bids, as with respect to any other interest therein, and shall have full authority to convey all the interest and rights acquired by any such bid or bids, purchase or purchases, to any corporation or corporations which may be formed for the purpose of holding and operating the said rail-road, or any part thereof, with such restrictions, conditions and agreements from the said corporation or corporations, as to the said purchasers or purchaser may seem expedient; and generally to do all acts and things for the formation of the said corporation or corporations, and for investing them when so formed with the rail-road property acquired by any such purchase or purchases.

And each of the persons subscribing hereto agrees to furnish his quota of the money necessary to defray the expenses and charges which may be incurred in the said sales or in the creation of the said corporation or corporations, or in the full carrying out of the agreements herein contemplated.

And it is further mutually agreed, that this agreement may be enforced as against any party hereto by action brought in the name of any person who may be designated by the said purchasers or purchaser for that purpose, or in the name of the corporation or corporations hereafter to be created, as herein provided, and that in case any party hereto shall fail to comply with all of the conditions and provisions of this agreement, the rights of such party, by virtue thereof, may, at the option of said purchasers or purchaser, or of the said corporation or corporations, be declared forfeited, and thereupon all interests of the said party, under or by virtue of this agreement, shall absolutely cease.

IN WITNESS WHEREOF, we have hereunto set our hands, on the 16th day of March, 1859, and have affixed opposite our names the number of bonds by us respectively subscribed hereto or to duplicates hereof.

THIS INDENTURE, made the second·day of June,·in the year of our Lord, one thousand eight hundred and fifty-nine, between James Winslow, of the City of Poughkeepsie, in the County of Dutchess and State of New-York, gentleman, party of the first part, and Samuel J. Tilden and Ossian D. Ashley, of the City and County and State of New-York, parties of the second part, .

Witnesseth, that, whereas The Chicago, St. Paul and Fond du Lac Rail-Road Company, a corporation existing under and by virtue of the laws of the States of Wisconsin and Illinois, did heretofore cause to be made, executed and delivered to the party of the first part hereto, then of the City, County and State of New-York, a certain deed of trust or indenture of mortgage bearing date on the first day of August, one thousand eight hundred and fifty-five, whereby the said Chicago, St. Paul and Fond du Lac Rail-Road Company granted, bargained, sold, conveyed and transferred, unto the said party of the first part hereto, and to his successor or successors, all and singular the rail-road of the said company, from Chicago, in the State of Illinois, *via* Woodstock, to Janesville, in the State of Wisconsin, and thence, *via* Watertown, to the City of Fond du Lac, in Wisconsin, together with all the rights of way, depot grounds, railways, rails, bridges, fences, stations, station-houses and other buildings, and all the lands and heredita-ments by the said company, then held in their name, or thereafter to be acquired in connection with their said rail-way, or relating thereto, whether obtained under the rights and privileges of their several charters, or conveyed to them by deed ; and also all the tolls, incomes, rents, issues and profits, and corporate. or other franchises of the said company, connected with their said line of railway, or re-lating thereto ; and also all the locomotive engines, tenders, cars of every kind, machinery, machine shops, tools, im-plements, wood and property connected with the proper equipment, working, operating and conducting of the said road then owned, or thereafter to be acquired by the said

2

company, for or appurtenant to the aforesaid line of road, in substitution of those then owned, or otherwise; all of which personal chattels were, by the said mortgage, declared to be fixtures and appurtenances to be used and sold therewith, and not separated therefrom. In trust, to have and to hold the same as security for the payment to the holders of certain bonds to be made and issued by the said Chicago, St. Paul and Fond du Lac Rail-Road Company, amounting in the aggregate to three millions of dollars; each of said bonds to be for the sum of one thousand dollars, and to be payable on the first day of August, in the year one thousand eight hundred and eighty-five, together with interest thereon, at the rate of seven per cent. per annum, to be paid semi-annually on the first day of February and August in each year, on presentation and surrender of the interest coupons annexed thereto, and each of said bonds to be substantially of the form set forth and contained in the said indenture of mortgage, and to contain a provision, that in case of the non-payment of interest for any half year, when demanded, and the same remaining in arrear for six months thereafter, the principal should become due and payable, on demand, from and after the date of such default, with interest then accrued and in arrear.

And whereas, in and by the said indenture, the said company did further covenant and agree to and with the said party of the first part hereto, the trustee in the said indenture of mortgage named, and his successor or successors in the trust thereby created, that for the further security and ultimate redemption of the said mortgage bonds to be issued by virtue of the said mortgage, they would annually, on or before the first of December in each year thereafter, beginning with the first day of December, one thousand eight hundred and fifty-eight, until the principal of said bonds was fully paid, set apart and appropriate from the earnings of the said road, for the preceding twelve months, and deposit with the aforesaid trustee, or his successor in the trust, the just and full sum of one and one-fourth per cent. (equal to $37,500 on $3,000,000) per annum, on all outstanding unconverted bonds, secured by said mortgage, which, together with the accumulation of interest thereon, would form a capital sufficient to pay and discharge the entire principal of all the mortgage bonds contemplated to be issued by virtue of the several provisions of said mortgage, on or before the maturity of the said bonds; the first setting apart and appropriation of said sinking fund to be made and deposited on the first day of December, Anno Domini one thousand eight hundred and fifty-eight; the said sinking fund or several sums of money thus.set apart and appropriated, with all accumulations of interest, to be laid out and invested by the said trustee; or his successor, in the manner provided in and by said indenture of mortgage, and applied to the payment and redemption of the said bonds at the maturity thereof.

And whereas it was in and by the said indenture further provided, that if the interest on any of the said bonds so to be issued should not be paid by the said company when the same should fall due, and if such interest should remain in arrear for six months, so that according to the general tenor of the said bonds the principal thereof should become demandable, or in case the said company should fail, neglect or refuse to set apart, appropriate and deposit with the said trustee or his successor the said several sums of money, or any or either of them, for the purpose of a sinking fund, at the times and in the manner particularly set forth and provided in the said mortgage, it should be lawful for the said trustee, the party of the first part hereto, and his successors in the trust, upon the request in writing of *bona fide* holders of said bonds to the aggregate amount of one hundred thousand dollars, to take possession of all and singular the said premises, property and franchises, so conveyed and transferred, or so expressed to be, and to sell the same at public auction to the highest bidder, on advertisement specifying the time and place of sale, published in three principal daily newspapers printed in the City of New-York, and in one such newspaper printed in the City of Chicago, and in one newspaper in each of the cities of Janesville and Fond du Lac, to be continued for sixty days immediately preceding said sale, or for such shorter time, not less than twenty days, as the said company might assent to, and to execute a proper, full and legal conveyance on the sale to the purchaser or purchasers thereof.

And whereas the said mortgage was duly recorded in the office of the Register of the several counties in the States of Wisconsin and Illinois respectively in which the property described in the said mortgage was situated.

And whereas the said Chicago, St. Paul and Fond du

Lac Rail-Road Company did, after the execution and delivery of said indenture of mortgage, proceed to issue the bonds described and provided for in the said indenture of mortgage, to the amount of three millions of dollars of said bonds, each of said bonds being in the form and containing the provisions specified in the said indenture of mortgage.

And whereas, after the issuing of said bonds by said company, default was made in the payment of the interest which fell due on certain of said bonds on the first day of August, one thousand eight hundred and fifty-seven, and of the interest which fell due on all said bonds on the first day of February, one thousand eight hundred and fifty-eight, and the first day of August, one thousand eight hundred and fifty-eight, and the first day of February, one thousand eight hundred and fifty-nine, and the said interest has remained in arrears and wholly unpaid.

And whereas the said company has wholly neglected and failed to set apart, appropriate or deposit with the said trustee, the party of the first part hereto, any of the several sums of money for the purposes of a sinking fund, required in and by the said indenture of mortgage to be set apart, appropriated and deposited with the said trustee, whereby and by reason whereof the entire principal of the said bonds has become due.

And whereas *bona fide* holders of the bonds secured by the said mortgage, to the aggregate amount of more than one hundred thousand dollars, have in writing requested the said party of the first part hereto, to enforce and exercise the powers of entry and sale contained in and conferred upon him by the said indenture of mortgage.

And whereas the said party of the first part hereto, upon such request in writing, and pursuant to the power and authority in him vested under and by virtue of the said indenture of mortgage, did, in the manner and for the time specified and provided in and by the said indenture of mortgage, advertise all and singular the premises, property and franchises described in and conveyed to him by the said indenture of mortgage, to be exposed for sale at public auction, to the highest bidder, at the Court House in the City of Janesville, Rock County, in the State of Wisconsin, on the second day of June, one thousand eight hundred and fifty-nine, at twelve o'clock at noon of that day.

And whereas the said party of the first part, in his capacity of trustee under said indenture of mortgage, did, on the second day of June, one thousand eight hundred and fifty-nine, at twelve o'clock at noon of that day, being the day and hour specified in the said advertisement at Janesville aforesaid, expose and offer for sale at public auction, all and singular the aforesaid premises, property and franchises, described in and conveyed to him by the said indenture of mortgage, at which said sale the said premises, property and franchises were struck off to the parties of the second part hereto, for the sum of two hundred thousand dollars, that being the highest sum bidden for the same.

Now this indenture witnesseth, that the said party of the first part to these presents, in order to carry into effect the sale so made by him as trustee as aforesaid, in consideration of the premises, and of the sum of money so bidden as aforesaid, the same being first duly paid by the parties of the second part, the receipt whereof is hereby acknowledged, hath granted, bargained and sold, and by these presents doth grant, bargain, sell and convey unto the said parties of the second part,

All the premises, property and franchises described and embraced in the said indenture of mortgage, to wit, all and singular the rail-road from Chicago, in the State of Illinois, via Woodstock, to Janesville, in the State of Wisconsin, and thence, via Watertown, to the City of Fond du Lac, in Wisconsin, being part of the rail-road known as the Chicago, St. Paul and Fond du Lac Rail-Road ; and the portions thereof from Chicago to Janesville, or about ninety-two miles, and from Fond du Lac to the La Crosse Junction, or about thirty miles, being completed and in operation ; and the portion thereof from Janesville to La Crosse Junction being partially constructed, together with all the rights of way, depot grounds, railways, rails, bridges, fences, stations, station-houses and other buildings ; and also all the lands and hereditaments of the said company, in connection with the said railway, or relating thereto ; and also all the tolls, incomes, rents, issues and profits, and corporate or other franchises of the said company connected with said line of railway, or relating thereto ; and also all the locomotive engines, tenders, cars of every kind, machinery, machine-shops, tools and implements, wood and property connected with the proper equipment, working and operating and conducting of the said road; and also all and singular the property of every name and nature, and all rights, privileges and franchises conveyed by or embraced within the said mortgage or deed of trust, it being intended by these presents to convey all the property, rights, privileges and franchises and things whatsoever which the said party of the first part, as trustee under and by virtue of the said deed or mortgage, may lawfully or rightfully sell and convey, and no more :

To have and to hold the same, to the said parties of the second part, as joint tenants, and not as tenants in common, and their assigns, and to the survivor of the survivor of the said parties, and to the heirs and assigns of such survivor, to the only proper use, benefit and behoof of them, the said parties of the second part, and of the survivor of the said parties, and of the heirs and assigns of such survivor forever, as fully and completely as the said party of the first part, by virtue of the indenture of mortgage or trust deed, holds, and by virtue of his powers as trustee, under the said indenture, can or could sell and convey the said premises, property and franchises, and not otherwise.

In witness whereof, the said party of the first part has hereunto set his hand and seal, the day and year first above written.

JAMES WINSLOW, [L. S.]
Trustee.

Sealed and delivered in the }
    presence of }

A. C. COVENTRY,
P. A. HOYNE.

STATE OF ILLINOIS, }
County of Cook, City of Chicago, } ss.

Be it remembered, that on this fourth day of June, in the year one thousand eight hundred and fifty-nine, before me, Philip A. Hoyne, a commissioner, resident in the City of Chicago, County of Cook and State of Illinois, duly commissioned and qualified by the executive authority and under the laws of the State of Wisconsin, to take the acknowledgment of deeds and other instruments of writing to be used or recorded in the said State of Wisconsin, personally appeared James Winslow, and acknowledged the foregoing conveyance to be his free act and deed for the uses and purposes therein contained, and that he does not wish to retract the same ; and I further certify, that I know the person who made the said acknowledgment to be the same individual described in and who executed the said conveyance.

    In witness whereof, I have hereunto set my hand [L. S.] and official seal, at Chicago, in said State and County, the day and year aforesaid.

PHILIP A. HOYNE,
A Commissioner for Wisconsin, in Illinois.

STATE OF ILLINOIS,   } ss.
County of Cook, City of Chicago, }

    Be it remembered, that on this fourth day of June, in the year one thousand eight hundred and fifty-nine, before me, the subscriber, a commissioner in and for said State of Illinois, appointed by the Governor of the State of Michigan to take the acknowledgment and proof of deeds and instruments of writing under seal, to be used and recorded in the said State of Michigan, and to administer oaths and affirmations, appeared James Winslow, and acknowledged that he had executed the foregoing instrument of writing for the uses and purposes therein mentioned ; and I further certify, that the person who made the said acknowledgment is known to me to be the individual described in and who executed the foregoing instrument.

    In testimony whereof, I have hereunto set my hand [L. S.] and official seal, the day and year above written, at Chicago, in the County of Cook and State of Illinois.

PHILIP A. HOYNE,
Commissioner for the State of
Michigan, in Illinois.

STATE OF ILLINOIS,   } ss.
County of Cook, City of Chicago, }

    I, Philip A. Hoyne, a Notary Public in and for the City of Chicago, in the County of Cook and State of Illinois, do hereby certify, that James Winslow, personally known to me as the same person whose name is subscribed to the foregoing instrument of writing, appeared before me this day in person, and acknowledged that he signed, sealed and delivered the said instrument of writing as his free and voluntary act, for the uses and purposes therein set forth.

L. S.]   Given under my hand and notarial seal, this fourth day of June, A. D. 1859.

PHILIP A. HOYNE,
Notary Public.

(Deed from William A. Booth and James F. D. Lanier to Samuel J. Tilden and Ossian D. Ashley.)

THIS INDENTURE, made the second day of June, in the year one thousand eight hundred and fifty-nine, between William A. Booth and James F. D. Lanier, of the City of New-York, in the State of New-York, parties of the first part, and Samuel J. Tilden and Ossian D. Ashley of the same city, parties of the second part, witnesseth, that whereas, the Chicago, St. Paul and Fond du Lac Rail-Road Company, a corporation existing under and by virtue of the laws of the States of Wisconsin, Michigan and Illinois, did heretofore cause to be made, executed and delivered to the parties of the first part hereto, and to one William B. Ogden, a certain trust deed or indenture of mortgage bearing date on the sixth day of April, in the year one thousand eight hundred and fifty-seven, whereby the said Chicago, St. Paul and Fond du Lac Rail-Road Company granted, bargained, sold, conveyed and transferred unto the said William A. Booth, James F. D. Lanier and William B. Ogden, as joint tenants, and not as tenants in common, and to their survivors or successors in the trust expressed in and created by said deed of trust, the entire rail-road of the said company from the City of Chicago through the cities of Janesville and Fond du Lac to Lake Superior, with two termini on said lake, one at or near Marquette, or the mouth of Carp River, and the other at or near Ontonagon, or the mouth of the Ontonagon River, being the direct lines between Chicago and said Marquette and Ontonagon, whether said lines be called and known as the Main Trunk lines, or some of them as branches to the Main Trunk line, and all the land, railways, rails, bridges, fences, right of way, stations, depot grounds, station houses and other buildings then held and owned, or which might thereafter be held or owned by said company, for the purpose of constructing, operating and maintaining their said rail-road, or the accommodation of the business thereof; and also all the tolls, income, rents, issues, profits and alienable franchises of the said company connected

with their rail-road or relating thereto; and also all the
locomotives or stationary engines, tenders and cars of every
kind, machinery, machine shops, tools and implements, and
materials connected with or intended for the construction,
equipment, operating and conducting of said rail-road, conveyed or intended to be conveyed in and by said trust
deed or indenture, then owned or thereafter to be acquired
by the said company, all of which were thereby declared
to be appurtenances and fixtures of said rail-road, and to
be used and sold therewith, and not separated therefrom;
and also all the right, title, interest, claim or demand which
the said company then had or thereafter should acquire in
or to one million of acres of public lands of the United
States, situated, lying and being in the States of Wisconsin
and Michigan, adjoining and adjacent to the above described
rail-road and branches between Fond du Lac and Lake
Winnebago, and Ontonagon and Marquette on Lake Superior, as in said indenture described, being parts and parcels of the lands which were granted to the States of Wisconsin and Michigan by Acts of Congress, approved June
3d, 1856, and by the said States of Wisconsin and Michigan
granted to the assignees and predecessors of said company,
and subsequently by consolidations conferred upon, assigned
to and confirmed in the said company as in the said indenture
is particularly set forth and described, in trust, to have and to
hold the same unto the said William A. Booth, James F. D.
Lanier and William B. Ogden, as joint tenants, and not as tenants in common, and their survivors or successors, as security
for the payment of the principal and interest of certain bonds
to be made and issued by the said Chicago, St. Paul and
Fond du Lac Rail-Road Company, either in the sum of one
thousand dollars or five hundred dollars, in series and parcels from time to time as might be required for the purposes in said indenture specified, and amounting in the aggregate to the sum of twelve million of dollars, if found necessary, all of said bonds to bear such rate of interest, with
coupons attached, as might be from time to time decided
upon, not to exceed the rate of eight per cent. per annum,
and all to become due to the holders thereof on the first
day of May, one thousand eight hundred and eighty-two,
and to stand equally and ratably secured by the said indenture, according to their respective amounts, without any
preference in respect to priority of date or time of issue.

And whereas, in and by the said indenture it was expressly provided and declared, that if the interest on the bonds so to be issued should not be paid by the said company when the same should fall due, and if there should be no moneys in the hands of the trustees out of which such interest might be paid, in accordance with the provisions of the said indenture, and if such interest should remain in arrear for three months, or if there should be a failure to pay the principal of said bonds, or any of them, or any part thereof when due and demandable, according to the tenor and effect thereof, at any time after such default, upon the request of the holders of two hundred and fifty thousand dollars in amount of said bonds, the said trustees or their successors, might and should enter upon and take possession of and sell all and singular the said premises, in and by the said indenture conveyed and transferred, or expressed or intended so to be, or so much or such parts thereof as they should deem necessary and proper, first giving notice by advertisement in two daily newspapers printed in the cities of Chicago and New-York, to be continued for four months or such shorter time, not less than forty days, as the said company might by resolution of its board of directors assent to.

And whereas it was in and by the said indenture further expressly provided and declared, in respect to all the right, title, interest, claim or demand which the said company then had, or thereafter might acquire in or to the one million of acres of public lands of the United States hereinbefore referred to as embraced in the said indenture, that if there should at any time be a default in the payment of interest or principal upon said bonds, and continue for three months after the same should be due, the said trustees should be, and they were, by the said indenture, authorized and empowered, in their discretion, to sell at public auction after notice published for three weeks in one or more newspapers in New-York, Chicago and Janesville, so much of said lands as might be necessary to pay and satisfy such liabilities, or that they might proceed in the manner by the said indenture authorized and provided in respect to the other property and franchises thereby conveyed.

And whereas the said indenture was duly recorded in the offices of the registers of the several counties in the

States of Wisconsin, Michigan and Illinois, respectively, in which the property or lands described or referred to in the said indenture were situated.

And whereas the said indenture, and the grant and conveyance therein contained, and the lien thereby created, were subject as to all that part of the rail-road of the said company from Chicago to Fond du Lac, and its appurtenances and franchises, to a prior lien of a certain indenture of mortgage bearing date the first day of August, one thousand eight hundred and fifty-five, made and executed by the said company to James Winslow, trustee, to secure the payment of the principal and interest of certain bonds issued by the said company, amounting in the aggregate to three millions of dollars, and subject, as to the right, title and interest of the said company, in and to the said one million acres of public lands, to the provisions and requirements of the before mentioned acts of Congress and the said acts of the legislatures of the States of Wisconsin and Michigan, respectively, granting the said lands to the assignors and predecessors of the said company.

And whereas, after the execution and delivery of the said indenture, the said Chicago, St. Paul and Fond du Lac Rail-Road Company proceeded to issue the bonds in and by the said indenture provided for and secured in manner and form as therein prescribed, to the amount of three millions of dollars, bearing interest at the rate of eight per cent. per annum, payable semi-annually.

And whereas, after the making, execution and delivery of said indenture, the said William B. Ogden, one of the trustees therein named, resigned as such trustee, and his said resignation has taken effect pursuant to the terms and provisions of the said indenture.

And whereas it was in and by the said indenture expressly provided, that any act or thing thereby required to be performed by the trustees therein named, or their successors, should be valid and binding if done or performed by any two of their number, except the appointment of agents or attorneys to convey lands.

And whereas, after the issuing of said bonds by the said company, default was made in the payment of the interest thereon, which fell due on the first day of November, one thousand eight hundred and fifty-seven, and of the interest which fell due thereon on the first day of May, one thousand

eight hundred and fifty-eight, and of the interest which fell
due thereon on the first day of November of the last mentioned year, and the said interest still remains in arrear
wholly due and unpaid.

And whereas the said parties hereto of the first part did,
on the first day of October, in the year one thousand eight
hundred and fifty-eight, enter into actual possession of the
said rail-road, and of all and singular the property and
premises described herein, and intended to be conveyed
hereby, and have ever since been, and at the time of the
execution and delivery hereof are in the actual possession
of the said rail-road property and premises.

And whereas *bona fide* holders of the said bonds, to the
aggregate amount of more than two hundred and fifty
thousand dollars, since default made in the payment of said
interest, have, in writing, requested the parties of the first
part hereto, the acting trustees under the aforesaid trust
deed or mortgage, to enforce and exercise the power of sale
conferred upon the trustees in and by the said deed or
mortgage.

And whereas the board of directors of the said The Chicago, St. Paul and Fond du Lac Rail-Road Company did,
by resolution, assent to a sale of the said rail-road and property conveyed by the said deed of trust or mortgage upon
notice by advertisement for a shorter time than four months,
(but not less than forty days,) as provided for in and by
the said deed of trust or mortgage.

And whereas the said parties of the first part hereto,
upon such request in writing, and pursuant to the power
and authority vested in them under and by virtue of said
deed of trust or mortgage, did, in the manner therein specified and provided, advertise all and singular the premises,
property and franchises described in and conveyed to the
said trustees by the said indenture, to be exposed for sale at
public auction to the highest bidder, at the Court House in
the City of Janesville, Rock County, in the State of Wisconsin, on the second day of June, one thousand eight hundred
and fifty-nine, at one o'clock in the afternoon of that day.

And whereas the said parties of the first part hereto, in
their capacity of trustees under said deed of trust or indenture of mortgage, did, on the said second day of June, one
thousand eight hundred and fifty-nine, at one o'clock in
the afternoon of that day, being the day and hour specified

in the said advertisement, at Janesville aforesaid, expose and offer for sale at public auction all and singular the aforesaid premises, property and franchises described in and conveyed to the said trustees by the said indenture, subject to the prior lien in respect to that part of the railroad of the said company from Chicago to Fond du Lac, and its appurtenances and franchises, created by the aforesaid trust deed or indenture of mortgage, to James Winslow, trustee, and all rights, acquired by any purchaser or purchasers under or by virtue of any sale made by the said James Winslow, trustee, under or in pursuance of the said last mentioned trust deed or indenture ; at which sale by the said parties of the first part hereto, all and singular the aforesaid premises, property and franchises were struck off to the said parties of the second part hereto, for the sum of forty thousand dollars, that being the highest sum bidden for the same.

Now, therefore, this indenture further witnesseth, that the said parties of the first part to these presents, in order to carry into effect the sale so made by them, as trustees as aforesaid, and in consideration of the premises and of the sum of money so bidden as aforesaid, the same being first duly paid by the said parties of the second part, the receipt whereof is hereby acknowledged, have granted, bargained and sold, and by these presents do grant, bargain, sell and convey unto the said parties of the second part, the rail-road of the said company from the City of Chicago through the cities of Janesville and Fond du Lac to Lake Superior, with two termini on said lake, one at or near Marquette, or the mouth of Carp River, and the other at or near Ontonagon, or the mouth of Ontonagon River, being the direct lines between Chicago and said Marquette and Ontonagon, whether said lines be called and known as the Main Trunk lines, or some of them as branches to the Main Trunk line. And all the land, railways, rails, bridges, fences, right of way, stations, depot grounds, station houses and other buildings held or owned by the said company, for the purpose of constructing, operating and maintaining their said rail-road or the accommodation of the business thereof, and also all the tolls, income, rents, issues, profits and alienable franchises of the said company, connected with their rail-road or relating thereto. And also all the locomotives or stationary engines, tenders and cars of every kind, machinery, machine shops, tools and implements, and materials connected with or intended for the construction or equipment, operating or conducting of said rail-road, conveyed or intended to be conveyed in and by the said deed of trust or indenture of mortgage to the said trustees, or which, at the time of the execution of said indenture, were owned or were thereafter acquired by the said company ; subject, nevertheless, as to all that part of the rail-road of the said company from Chicago to Fond du Lac, and its appurtenances, property and franchises, to the prior lien of the aforesaid indenture of mortgage, made and executed by the said company to James Winslow, trustee, and to all rights and claims which may have been acquired by any person, persons or corporations under or by virtue of any sale, grant or conveyance made by the said James Winslow, trustee, under or by virtue of such indenture of mortgage. And also all the right, title, interest, claim or demand which the said company may have acquired in or to one million of acres of public lands of the United States, situated, lying and being in the States of Wisconsin and Michigan, adjoining and adjacent to the above described rail-road and branches between Fond du Lac, on Lake Winnebago, and Ontonagon and Marquette, on Lake Superior, as in said indenture made to said trustees is described, being parts and parcels of the lands which were granted to the States of Wisconsin and Michigan by the Acts of Congress approved June 3d, 1856, in the said indenture referred to, together with all and singular the tenements, hereditaments and appurtenances thereunto belonging, or in any wise appertaining ; subject, nevertheless, to the provisions and requirements of the several acts of Congress aforesaid, and the acts of the legislatures of the States of Wisconsin and Michigan, respectively granting the said lands to the assignors and predecessors of the said company. And also all and singular the property of every name and nature, and all rights, privileges and franchises conveyed by or embraced within the said indenture made to the said trustees, the said parties of the first part, and the said William B. Ogden as aforesaid. It being intended by these presents to convey all the property, rights, privileges and franchises, and things whatsoever which the said parties of the first part, as trustees, under and by virtue of the said last mentioned indenture, may or might lawfully or rightfully sell and convey, and no more.

To have and to hold the same to the said parties of the second part, as joint tenants and not as tenants in common, and their assigns, and to the survivor of the said parties, and the heirs and assigns of such survivors, to and for the only proper use of them, the said parties of the second part, and their assigns, and of the survivor of the said parties, and of the heirs and assigns of such survivor forever, as fully and completely as the said parties of the first part, by virtue of the said indenture made to them and the said William B. Ogden as aforesaid, hold, and of their powers as trustees under the same can or could sell and convey the said premises, property and franchises, and not otherwise.

In witness whereof, the said parties of the first part hereto have hereunto set their hands and seals the day and year first above written.

WM. A. BOOTH,   [L. S.]
Trustee.

JAMES F. D. LANIER,   [L. S.]
Trustee.

Sealed and delivered in }
   presence of   }

      A. C. COVENTRY.
      P. A. HOYNE.

STATE OF ILLINOIS,   }
County of Cook, City of Chicago, } ss.

Be it remembered, that on this fourth day of June, in the year one thousand eight hundred and fifty-nine, before me, Philip A. Hoyne, a commissioner, resident in the City of Chicago, County of Cook and State of Illinois, duly commissioned and qualified by the executive authority, and under the laws of the State of Wisconsin, to take acknowledgment of deeds and other instruments of writing to be used and recorded in the said State of Wisconsin, personally appeared WILLIAM A. BOOTH and JAMES F. D. LANIER, and severally acknowledged the foregoing conveyance to be their free act and deed, for the uses and purposes therein contained, and that they do not wish to retract the same. And I further certify that I know the persons who made the said acknowledgment to be the same individuals described in and who executed the said conveyance.

In witness whereof, I have hereunto set my hand
[L. S.]   and official seal at Chicago, in said State and
County, the day and year aforesaid.

PHILIP A. HOYNE,
A Commissioner for the State of
Wisconsin, in Illinois.

STATE OF ILLINOIS,   } ss.
County of Cook, City of Chicago, }

Be it remembered, that on this fourth day of June, in
the year one thousand eight hundred and fifty-nine, before
me, the subscriber, a commissioner in and for said State of
Illinois, appointed by the Governor of the State of Michigan to take the acknowledgment and proof of deeds and
instruments of writing under seal, to be used and recorded
in the said State of Michigan, and to administer oaths and
affirmations, appeared WILLIAM A. BOOTH and JAMES F.
D. LANIER, and severally acknowledged that they had executed the foregoing instrument of writing for the uses and
purposes therein contained. And I further certify, that
the persons who made the said acknowledgment are known
to me to be the individuals described in and who executed
the foregoing instrument.

In testimony whereof, I have hereunto set my hand
[L. S.]   and official seal, the day and year above written,
at Chicago, in the County of Cook and State of
Illinois.

PHILIP A. HOYNE,
A Commissioner for the State of
Michigan, in Illinois.

STATE OF ILLINOIS,   } ss.
Cook County, City of Chicago, }

I, PHILIP A. HOYNE, a Notary Public in and for the City
of Chicago, in the County and State aforesaid, do hereby
certify that WILLIAM A. BOOTH and JAMES F. D. LANIER,
personally known to me as the same persons whose names
are subscribed to the annexed instrument of writing, appeared before me this day in person, and acknowledged
that they signed, sealed and delivered the said instrument
of writing as their free and voluntary act for the uses and
purposes therein set forth.

Given under my hand and notarial seal, this 4th day of
June, A. D. 1859.

[L. S.]   PHILIP A. HOYNE.

(Deed from William B. Ogden to Samuel J. Tilden and Ossian D. Ashley.)

THIS INDENTURE, made this second day of June, in the year one thousand eight hundred and fifty-nine, between WILLIAM B. OGDEN, of the City of Chicago in the State of Illinois, of the first part, and SAMUEL J. TILDEN and OSSIAN D. ASHLEY, of the City and State of New-York, of the second part.

Whereas the said party of the first part, together with William A. Booth and James F. D. Lanier, of the City and State of New-York, was a trustee under and by virtue of a trust deed or mortgage, made and delivered by the Chicago, St. Paul and Fond du Lac Rail-Road Company, bearing date on the sixth day of April, 1857, and recorded in the Recorder's office for Cook County, Illinois, June 6, 1857, in Book 134 of Deeds, page 596, &c.; for Lake County, June 27, 1857, in Book P. of Mortgages, page 605, &c.; for McHenry County, June 8, 1857, in Volume 12 of Mortgages, page 571, &c.; and for Boone County, June 25, 1857, in Book I. of Mortgages, page 582, &c.; and in the Register's office for the County of Walworth in the State of Wisconsin, June 24, 1857, in Volume 19 of Mortgages, page 400, &c.; for Rock County, June 8, 1857, in Volume 4 of Mortgages, page 39, &c.; for Jefferson County, June 9, 1857, in Volume 18 of Mortgages; for Dodge County, June 20, 1857, in Volume S. of Mortgages, page 306, &c.; for Fond du Lac County, June 10, 1857, in Volume 14 of Deeds, page 200, &c.; for Winnebago County, June 12, 1857, in Book 8 of Mortgages, page 1, &c.; for Outagamie County, June 13, 1857, in Volume 3 of Mortgages, page 500, &c.; for Waupacca County, June 30, 1857, in Volume 1 of Mortgages, page 234, &c.; for Brown County, June 13, 1857, in Volume 8 of Mortgages, page 441, &c.; and for Oconto County, June 15, 1857, in Volume A. of Mortgages; and in the office of the Secretary of State for the State of Wisconsin, May 18, 1857, in Book of R. R. Mortgages, page 178, &c.; in the Recorder's office for Marquette County, Michigan, June 13, 1857, in Book 1 of Mortgages, page 124, &c.; and for Ontonagon County,

June 11, 1857, in Liber A. of Mortgages, folio 221, &c., which said trust deed conveyed to the said trustees all and singular the entire rail-road of the said company and its appurtenances, and the locomotives, cars, machinery, tools and fixtures, and also certain lands and land grants given and granted to said company for the construction of its line of road, and all privileges, franchises and rights, and the other property and things hereinafter mentioned, for the purpose of securing the payment of the interest and principal of certain bonds in the said trust deed described.

And whereas it was provided in and by the said trust deed, that any of the said trustees might resign, to take effect after sixty days' notice, in writing, shall have been given to the president or secretary of said rail-road company, and the said party of the first part did, on or before the thirty-first day of March, in the year 1859, in conformity to the said provision, resign as such trustee.

And whereas it was further provided in and by the said trust deed, that the powers of entry, sale and conveyance thereby granted to the said trustees, in case of default in the said trust deed specified, might be exercised by any two of the said trustees, as validly and effectually as if all joined, and also provided that in case of a vacancy in the number of the said trustees by resignation, the remaining trustees should, while such vacancy continued, exercise all the powers conferred upon the trustees.

And whereas, in pursuance of the powers and authorities in and by the said trust deed granted, the said William A. Booth and James F. D. Lanier, the continuing trustees, did, on the second day of June, 1859, sell at public auction, held in the City of Janesville, in the State of Wisconsin, all and singular the premises, franchises, rights and things in the said trust deed described, unto the parties of the second part, and did thereupon execute and deliver to the said parties a conveyance of the same.

And whereas the said party of the first part, not having released the legal estate in the said premises, franchises, rights and things to the said continuing trustees, has been requested by them to execute and deliver such release directly to the parties hereto of the second part, as the purchasers and grantees from the said continuing trustees, as well for the purpose of attesting the fact of the said resignation of the party of the first part, as for the further assuring of the said legal estate unto the said purchasers and grantees.

Now, therefore, this indenture witnesseth, that the said party of the first part, in consideration of the premises and of one dollar to him in hand paid by the said parties of the second part, does grant, bargain, sell, remise, release and convey unto the parties of the second part all the estate, right, title and interest which the said party of the first part has, or might have, as a trustee, with the said William A. Booth and James F. D. Lanier, under or by virtue of the aforesaid trust deed of the said Chicago, St. Paul and Fond du Lac Rail-Road Company, hereinbefore referred to, of, in and to all and singular the premises, lands, hereditaments, franchises, rights and things in the said trust deed mentioned ; and all and singular the premises, lands, hereditaments, franchises, rights and things in the aforesaid conveyance from the said William A. Booth and James F. D. Lanier to the parties of the second part mentioned, which said trust deed and which said conveyance are hereby referred to for the purpose of a fuller description of the rights and things intended to be hereby conveyed.

To have and to hold unto the said parties of the second part, as joint tenants, and not as tenants in common, and to their assigns, and the survivor of the said parties of the second part, and the heirs and assigns of such survivor, to and for the proper use and behoof of the said parties and their assigns, and of the survivor and the heirs and assigns of such survivor, as fully and completely as the said party of the first part can or could, as such trustee, convey the said premises, lands, hereditaments, franchises and things, and not otherwise.

In witness whereof, the said party of the first part hath hereunto set his hand and seal, the day and year first above written.

W. B. Ogden. [l. s.]

Signed, sealed and delivered }
    in presence of   }

James R. Young,
Finley J. Wright.

UNITED STATES OF AMERICA, ⎫
    State of New-York, ⎬ ss.
· *City and County of New-York,* ⎭

Be it known, that on the seventh day of October, in the year one thousand eight hundred and fifty-nine, before me, the undersigned, Edwin F. Corey, Junior, resident in the City of New-York, and a commissioner duly commissioned and qualified by the executive authority, and under the laws of the State of Wisconsin, to take the acknowledgment of deeds, &c., to be used or recorded therein, and a commissioner duly commissioned and qualified by the executive authority, and under the laws of the State of Michigan, to take the acknowledgment of deeds, &c., to be used or recorded therein, and a Public Notary in and for the State of New-York, by Letters Patent, under the Great Seal of State, duly commissioned and sworn, personally appeared William B. Ogden, to me personally known to be the real person described in, and who executed the foregoing instrument of writing, and acknowledged that he executed the same as his free, voluntary act and deed, for the uses and purposes therein set forth, and did not wish to retract the same. And I hereby certify, that the said instrument is executed and acknowledged according to the laws of the State of New-York.

In testimony whereof, I have hereunto set my hand and affixed my seals of office, as such Notary and Commissioner, at my office, in the City of New-York, the day and year first above written.

[L. S.]   [L. S.]   EDWIN F. COREY, JU'R,

       Commissioner for the States of Wisconsin
[L. S.]   *and Michigan, and Notary Public in*
           and for the State of New-York.

(Deed from Chicago, St. Paul and Fond du Lac Rail-Road Company to Samuel J. Tilden and Ossian D. Ashley.)

THIS INDENTURE, made this thirtieth day of June, in the year one thousand eight hundred and fifty-nine, between the CHICAGO, ST. PAUL AND FOND DU LAC RAIL-ROAD COMPANY, a corporation existing under and by virtue of the laws of the States of Illinois, Wisconsin and Michigan, of the first part, and SAMUEL J. TILDEN and OSSIAN D. ASHLEY, of the City and State of New-York, of the second part.

Whereas the said party of the first part executed and delivered to James Winslow, of the City and State of New-York, a trust deed or mortgage, bearing date on the first day of August, 1855, and recorded in the Register's Office for Cook County, Illinois, August 14, 1855, in Book 21 of Mortgages, page 376, &c.; for Lake County, August 15, 1855, in Book O., page 1, &c.; for McHenry County, August 15, 1855, in Book 10, page 49, &c.; and for Boone County, August 16, 1855, in Book J., page 44, &c.; and in the Register's Office for the County of Walworth, in the State of Wisconsin, August 24, 1855, in Volume 15 of Mortgages, page 589, &c.; for Rock County, August 16, 1855, in Volume R., page 432, &c.; for Jefferson County, August 17, 1855, Volume 13, page 180, &c.; for Dodge County, August 22, 1855, in Volume N., page 142, &c.; for Fond du Lac County, August 20, 1855, in Volume P., page 120, &c.; which said trust deed conveyed all and singular the rail-road and its appurtenances, and the locomotives, cars, machinery, tools and fixtures, and also the privileges, franchises and rights, and the other property and things hereinafter mentioned, for the purpose of securing the payment of the interest and principal of certain bonds in the said trust deed described.

And whereas the said party of the first part also executed and delivered to William A. Booth and James F. D. Lanier, of the City of New-York, and William B. Ogden, of the City of Chicago, trustees, a trust deed or mortgage, bearing date on the sixth day of April, 1857, and recorded in the Recorder's Office for Cook County, Illinois, June

6th, 1857, in Book 134 of Deeds, page 596, &c.; for Lake County, June 27, 1857, in Book P. of Mortgages, page 605, &c.; for McHenry County, June 8, 1857, in Volume 12 of Mortgages, page 571, &c.; and for Boone County, June 25, 1857, in Book I. of Mortgages, page 582, &c.; and in the Register's Office for the County of Walworth, in the State of Wisconsin, June 24, 1857, in Volume 19 of Mortgages, page 400, &c.; for Rock County, June 8, 1857, in Volume 4 of Mortgages, page 39, &c.; for Jefferson County, June 9, 1857, in Volume 18 of Mortgages; for Dodge County, June 20, 1857, in Volume S. of Mortgages, page 306, &c.; for Fond du Lac County, June 10, 1857, in Volume 14 of Deeds, page 200, &c.; for Winnebago County, June 12, 1857, in Book 8 of Mortgages, page 1, &c.; for Outagamie County, June 13, 1857, in Volume 3 of Mortgages, page 500, &c.; for Waupacca County, June 30, 1857, in Volume 1 of Mortgages, page 234, &c.; for Brown County, June 13, 1857, in Volume S of Mortgages, page 441, &c.; and for Oconto County, June 15, 1857, in Volume A. of Mortgages; and in the office of the Secretary of State for the State of Wisconsin, May 18, 1857, in Book of R. R. Mortgages, page 178, &c.; in the Recorder's Office for Marquette County, Michigan, June 13, 1857, in Book 1 of Mortgages, page 124, &c.; and for Ontonagon County, June 11, 1857, in Liber A. of Mortgages, folio 221, &c.; which said trust deed conveyed to the said trustees all and singular the entire rail-road of the said company, and its appurtenances, and the locomotives, cars, machinery, tools and fixtures, and also certain lands and land grants given and granted to said company for the construction of its line of road, and all privileges, franchises and rights, and the other property and things hereinafter mentioned, for the purpose of securing the payment of the interest and principal of certain bonds in the said trust deed described.

And whereas default was made in the conditions of both of the said trust deeds, and in pursuance of the powers and authorities therein contained, the said James Winslow, trustee under the said trust deed first mentioned, and the said William A. Booth and James F. D. Lanier, continuing trustees under the said trust deed last mentioned, did, on the second day of June, 1859, sell at public auction, held at the City of Janesville, all and singular the lands, hereditaments, property, franchises, rights and things, in the said trust deeds described, to the parties hereto of the second part, and did, by deeds bearing date on that day, convey the same unto the said parties of the second part.

And whereas the said parties of the second part have organized, in pursuance of a statute of the State of Wisconsin, entitled "An act to facilitate and authenticate the formation of a corporation by the purchasers of the Chicago, St. Paul and Fond ·du Lac Rail-Road Company," approved March 14, 1859, and a statute of the State of Illinois, entitled "An act to authorize the sale of the Chicago, St. Paul and Fond du Lac Rail-Road, and to enable the purchasers thereof to form a corporation," approved February 19th, 1859, and of the laws of the said States, a corporation under the name of the Chicago and North Western Railway Company, and are about to convey the aforesaid railway, property, franchises, rights and things to the said corporation.

Now this indenture witnesseth, that the said party of the first part, in consideration of the premises, and of one dollar to the said party of the first part paid by the parties of the second part, has granted, bargained, sold, remised, released and conveyed, and does by these presents, grant, bargain, sell, remise, release and convey unto the said parties of the second part, all and singular the railways, ways and rights of way, depot grounds and other lands; all tracks, bridges, viaducts, culverts, fences and other structures; all depots, station houses, engine houses, car houses, freight houses, wood houses and other buildings; and all machine shops and other shops required for use, in connection with the said railway or the business thereof; and including, also, all locomotives, tenders, cars and other rolling stock or equipment, and all machinery, tools, implements and materials for the constructing, operating, repairing or replacing the said railway, or any part thereof, or any of its equipment or appurtenances; and also all the franchises connected with or relating to the said railway, or the construction, maintenance or use thereof, and all corporate and other franchises, and all property, rights or things granted or conveyed, or expressed or intended so to be by the aforesaid trust deeds, or either of them, for a more particular description of which reference is made to the said trust deeds, as well as to the aforesaid conveyances of the said James Winslow, and of the said William A. Booth and James F. D. Lanier, to the said parties of the second part : Together with all and singular the tenements, hereditaments and appurtenances thereunto belonging, or in any wise appertaining, and the reversions, remainders, tolls, incomes, rents, issues and profits thereof; and also all the estate, right, title, interest, property, possession, claim and demand whatsoever, as well in law as in equity of the said party of the first part, of, in and to the same, and any and every part thereof, with the appurtenances. To have and to hold the same unto the said parties of the second part, and their assigns, as joint tenants, and not as tenants in common, and unto the survivor of the said parties, of and for the only proper use and behoof of the said parties of the second part and their assigns, and of the survivor of them, and the heirs and assigns of such survivor, forever.

In testimony whereof, the said party of the first part has caused its common and corporate seal to be hereto affixed, and the same to be attested by the signature of its president and treasurer, and the parties of the second part have hereunto set their hands and seals the day and year first before written.

[L. S.]　W. B. OGDEN, *President.*
　　　　CHARLES BUTLER,
　　　　　　Treasurer and Secretary.

Signed, sealed and delivered ⎱
　　in presence of　　　⎰
　　　JAMES R. YOUNG,
　　　FINLEY J. WRIGHT.

UNITED STATES OF AMERICA, ⎱
　　State of New-York,　　⎰ ss.
　City and County of New-York, ⎰

Be it known, that on the seventh day of October, in the year one thousand eight hundred and fifty-nine, before me, the undersigned, Edwin F. Corey, Junior, resident in the City of New-York, and a commissioner duly commissioned and qualified by the executive authority, and under the laws of the State of Wisconsin, to take the acknowledgment of deeds, &c., to be used or recorded therein, and a commissioner duly commissioned and qualified by the executive authority, and under the laws of the State of Michigan, to take the acknowledgment of deeds, &c., to be used or recorded therein, and a public notary in and for the State of New-York, by Letters Patent under the Great Seal of State, duly commissioned and sworn, personally appeared William B. Ogden and Charles Butler, to me personally known to be the real persons described in and who executed the foregoing instrument. And the said William B. Ogden being by me duly sworn, said, that he resides in the City of Chicago, State of Illinois, and that he is the President of the Chicago, St. Paul and Fond du Lac Rail-Road Company, that the seal affixed to the foregoing instrument is the common and corporate seal of said company, and was affixed thereto by their authority, and that he, as president, and Charles Butler, as secretary and treasurer, subscribed their names thereto, by the like authority, and that said Charles Butler is the secretary and treasurer of said company.

And said Charles Butler acknowledged that he executed said instrument on behalf of and as the act and deed of the said rail-road company, for the uses and purposes therein mentioned.

And I hereby certify that the said instrument is executed and acknowledged according to the laws of the State of New-York.

In testimony whereof, I have hereunto set my hand, and affixed my seals of office as such notary and commissioner, at my office in the City of New-York, the day and year first above written.

[L. S.]   [L. S.]   EDWIN F. COREY, JU'R,
Commissioner for the States of Wisconsin
[L. S.]   *and Michigan, and Notary Public for*
the State of New-York.

(Deed from Samuel J. Tilden and Ossian D. Ashley to the Chicago and North Western Railway Company.)

THIS INDENTURE, made this first day of July, in the year of our Lord one thousand eight hundred and fifty-nine, between SAMUEL J. TILDEN and OSSIAN D. ASHLEY, of the City and State of New-York, parties of the first part, and the CHICAGO AND NORTH WESTERN RAILWAY COMPANY, party of the second part, and HARRIET A. ASHLEY, wife of the said Ossian D. Ashley, party of the third part, witnesseth, that

Whereas the said parties of the first part became the purchasers of a certain railway hereinafter more particularly described, and formerly known as the Chicago, St. Paul and Fond du Lac Rail-Road, and of certain other property and franchises formerly owned or possessed by the Chicago, St. Paul and Fond du Lac Rail-Road Company, at sales by public auction, duly made at Janesville, in the State of Wisconsin, on the second day of June, 1859, by virtue of a certain mortgage or trust deed of the said company, bearing date on the first day of August, one thousand eight hundred and fifty-five, and recorded in the Register's office for Cook County, Illinois, August 14th, 1855, in Book 21 of Mortgages, page 376, &c.; for Lake County, August 15th, 1855, in Book O., page 1, &c.; for McHenry County, August 15th, 1855, in Book 10, page 49, &c.; and for Boone County, August 16th, 1855, in Book J., page 44, &c.; and in the Register's office for the County of Walworth, in the State of Wisconsin, August 24th, 1855, in Volume 15 of Mortgages, page 589, &c.; for Rock County, August 16th, 1855, in Volume R., page 432, &c.; for Jefferson County, August 17th, 1855, Volume 13, page 180, &c.; for Dodge County, August 22nd, 1855, in Volume N., page 142, &c.; for Fond du Lac County, August 20th, 1855, in Volume P., page 120, &c.; and of a certain other mortgage or trust deed of the said company, bearing date on the sixth day of April, one thousand eight hundred and fifty-seven, and recorded in the Recorder's office for Cook County, Illinois, June 6th, 1857, in Book 134 of Deeds, page 596, &c,; for Lake County, June 27th, 1857, in Book P. of

Mortgages, page 605, &c.; for McHenry County, June 8th, 1857, in Volume 12 of Mortgages, page 571, &c.; and for Boone County, June .25th, 1857, in Book I. of Mortgages, page 582, &c.; and in the Register's office for the County of Walworth, in the State of Wisconsin, June 24th, 1857, in Volume 19 of Mortgages, page 400, &c.; for Rock County, June 8th, 1857, in Volume 4 of Mortgages, page 39, &c.; for Jefferson County, June 9th, 1857, in Volume 18 of Mortgages; for Dodge County, June 20th, 1857, in Volume 8. of Mortgages, page 306, &c.; for Fond du Lac County, June 10th, 1857, in Volume 14 of Deeds, page 200, &c.; for Winnebago County, June 12th, 1857, in Book 8 of Mortgages, page 1, &c.; for Outagamie County, June 13th, 1857, in Volume 3 of Mortgages, page 500, &c.; for Waupacca County, June 30th, 1857, in Volume 1 of Mortgages, page 234, &c.; for Brown County, June 13th, 1857, in Volume 8 of Mortgages, page 441, &c.; and for Oconto County, June 15th, 1857, in Volume A. of Mortgages; and in the office of the Secretary of State for the State of Wisconsin, May 18th, 1857, in Book of R. R. Mortgages, page 178, &c.; in the Recorder's office for Marquette County, Michigan, June 13th, 1857, in Book 1 of Mortgages, page 124, &c., and for Ontonagon County, June 11th, 1857, in liber A. of Mortgages, folio 221, &c.

And whereas James Winslow, trustee under the said mortgage or trust deed of the said Chicago, St. Paul and Fond du Lac Rail-Road Company, bearing date the first day of August, one thousand eight hundred and fifty-five, did, by deed bearing date the said second day of June, one thousand eight hundred and fifty-nine, and duly executed and delivered to the said parties hereto of the first part, convey unto the said parties the property, franchises and things therein described, as follows: All and singular the rail-road from Chicago, in the State of Illinois, *via* Woodstock to Janesville, in the State of Wisconsin, and thence *via* Watertown to the City of Fond du Lac, in Wisconsin, being part of the rail-road known as the Chicago, St. Paul and Fond du Lac Rail-Road, and the portions thereof from Chicago to Janesville, or about ninety-two miles, and from Fond du Lac to the La Crosse Junction, or about thirty miles, being completed and in operation, and the portion thereof from Janesville to La Crosse Junction being partially constructed, together with all the rights of way, depot grounds, railways, rails, bridges, fences, stations, station houses and other buildings; and also all the lands and hereditaments of the said company, in connection with the said railway, or relating thereto; and also all the tolls, income, rents, issues and profits, and corporate or other franchises of the said Chicago, St. Paul and Fond du Lac Rail-Road Company, connected with the said line of railway, or relating thereto; and also all the locomotive engines, tenders, cars of every kind, machinery, machine shops, tools and implements, wood and property connected with the proper equipment, working and operating and conducting of the said road; and also all and singular the property of every name and nature, and all rights, privileges and franchises conveyed by, or embraced within the said mortgage or deed of trust; it being intended, by these presents, to convey all the property, rights, privileges and franchises and things whatsoever, which the said party of first part, as trustee, under and by virtue of the said deed or mortgage, may lawfully or rightfully sell and convey, and no more.

And whereas William A. Booth and James F. D. Lanier, the continuing trustees under the said mortgage or trust deed of the said Chicago St. Paul and Fond du Lac Rail-Road Company, made to the said trustees with William B. Ogden, who has since resigned, and bearing date the sixth day of April, one thousand eight hundred and fifty-seven, did, by deed bearing date the said (2d) second day of June, one thousand eight hundred and fifty-nine, and duly executed and delivered to the said parties hereto of the first part, convey unto the said parties the property, franchises and things therein described as follows:

The rail-road of the said Chicago, St. Paul and Fond du Lac Rail-Road Company, from the City of Chicago through the cities of Janesville and Fond du Lac to Lake Superior, with two termini on the said lake, one at or near Marquette, or the mouth of Carp River, and the other at or near Ontonagon, or the mouth of Ontonagon River, being the direct lines between Chicago and said Marquette and Ontonagon, whether said lines be called and known as the Main Trunk Lines, or some of them as branches to the Main Trunk Line; and all the land, railways, rails, bridges, fences, right of way, stations, depot grounds, station houses and other buildings held or owned by the said company for the purpose of constructing, operating and maintaining their said rail-road or the accommodation of the business thereof; and also all the tolls, income, rents, issues, profits and alienable franchises of the said company, connected with their rail-road or relating thereto; and also all the locomotives or stationary engines, tenders and cars of every kind, machinery, machine shops, tools and implements, and materials connected with or intended for the construction or equipment, operating or conducting of said rail-road, conveyed or intended to be conveyed, in and by the said deed of trust or indenture of mortgage to the said trustees, or which, at the time of the execution of said indenture, were owned or were thereafter acquired by the said company: subject, nevertheless, as to all that part of the rail-road of the said company from Chicago to Fond du Lac, and its appurtenances, property and franchises, to the prior lien of the aforesaid indenture of mortgage, made and executed by the said company to James Winslow, trustee, and to all rights and claims which may have been acquired by any person, persons or corporations under or by virtue of any sale, grant or conveyance made by the said James Winslow, trustee, under or by virtue of such indenture of mortgage; and also, all the right, title, interest, claim or demand, which the said company may have acquired in or to one million of acres of public lands of the United States, situated, lying and being in the States of Wisconsin and Michigan, adjoining and adjacent the above described rail-road and branches between Fond du Lac, on Lake Winnebago, and Ontonagon and Marquette, on Lake Superior, as in said indenture made to said trustees is described, being parts and parcels of the lands which were granted to the States of Wisconsin and Michigan by the acts of Congress, approved June 3d, 1856, in the said indenture referred to, together with all and singular the tenements, hereditaments, and appurtenances thereunto belonging or in any wise appertaining; subject, nevertheless, to the provisions and requirements of the several acts of Congress aforesaid, and the acts of the legislatures of the States of Wisconsin and Michigan respectively, granting the said lands to the assignors and predecessors of the said company; and also all and singular the property of every name and nature; and all rights, privileges and franchises conveyed by or embraced within the said indenture made to the said trustees, the said parties of the first part, and the said William B. Ogden, as aforesaid ; it being intended by these presents to convey all the property, rights, privileges and franchises and things whatsoever, which the said parties of the first part, as trustees under and by virtue of the said last mentioned indenture, may or might lawfully or rightfully sell and convey, and no more.

And whereas the party hereto of the second part is a corporation duly formed and organized in pursuance of an act of the State of Wisconsin, entitled "An act to facilitate and authenticate the formation of a corporation by the purchasers of the Chicago, St. Paul and Fond du Lac Rail-Road Company," approved March 14th, 1859, and of the laws of the State of Wisconsin, and is also a corporation duly formed and organized in pursuance of an act of the State of Illinois, entitled, "An act to authorize the sale of the Chicago, St. Paul and Fond du Lac Rail-Road, and to enable the purchasers thereof to form a corporation," approved February 19th, 1859; and the laws of the State of Illinois.

And whereas the said parties hereto of the first part have agreed to and with the said party of the second part to sell and convey to the said party of the second part all and singular the property, franchises and things conveyed to the said parties of the first part by the aforesaid deeds of the said James Winslow, and of the said William A. Booth and James F. D. Lanier, in consideration of the making and delivery by the said party of the second part to the said parties of the first part, of certain bonds and stock of the said party of the second part, the nature, forms, amounts and denominations of which are more particularly described and fixed in an agreement between the parties hereto, bearing even date herewith.

Now, therefore, in consideration of the premises, and of the making and delivering to the said parties of the first part of the aforesaid bonds and stock, and of one dollar, the receipt whereof is hereby acknowledged, the parties hereto of the first part and the party hereto of the third part have granted, bargained, sold, assigned, transferred and set over, and do by these presents grant, bargain, sell, convey, assign, transfer and set over unto the said party hereto of the second part, all the right, title and interest of

them, the parties of the first and third parts, and of either
of the said parties acquired by virtue of the deeds of the
said James Winslow, trustee, or by virtue of the deed of
the said William A. Booth and James F. D. Lanier, trustees, both of which deeds bear date the second day of
June, 1859, and are herein before referred to and in part
recited, of, in and to all and singular the rail-roads and
their appurtenances, and all the estates, real, personal or
mixed, and all the property, franchises, rights and
things of whatever name or nature, which are embraced
in or conveyed by the aforesaid deeds of the said
Winslow and the said Booth and Lanier, for a more
particular description of which reference is made to
the said deeds, and the parts thereof hereinbefore recited,
and all right, title and interest of them, the parties of the
first and third parts, and of either of them, acquired by
virtue of a conveyance made by William B. Ogden, a
former trustee, under the said second or Land Grant Mortgage or Trust Deed, to the parties of the first part, and bearing date the second day of June, one thousand eight hundred and fifty-nine, or acquired by virtue of a conveyance
made by the Chicago, St. Paul and Fond du Lac Rail-
Road Company to the parties of the first part, and bearing
date the thirtieth day of June, one thousand eight hundred
and fifty-nine. Provided, nevertheless, and it is the true
intent and meaning of these presents, that nothing herein
contained shall be construed to express or imply any covenant by the parties of the first or third parts, or either of
them, but that this instrument shall operate to convey, in
behalf of the said parties, all the estates and interests in
the railway and appurtenances, property, rights, franchises
and things hereinbefore described, which the said parties or
either of them might hold by virtue of the aforesaid conveyances, and which the said parties, each for himself or
herself, and not one for the other, can lawfully and rightfully convey, and no more.

To have and to hold the same unto the said party of the
second part, and its successors and assigns, to and for its
and their own proper use, benefit and behoof, forever, as
fully as the said parties of the first and third parts can
convey the same, as aforesaid, and not otherwise.

And the said party of the third part, wife of the said
Ossian D. Ashley, one of the parties of the first part, for

the considerations aforesaid, and of one dollar to her in hand paid, the receipt whereof from the party of the second part is hereby acknowledged, has joined with her said husband in these presents, and has released, and does hereby release unto the said party of the second part, all her right and title of dower in all and singular the premises hereinbefore granted.

In witness whereof, the said parties hereto, of the first and third parts, have hereunto set their hands and seals, on the day and year first above written.

SAMUEL J. TILDEN, [L. S.]
O. D. ASHLEY, [L. S.]
HARRIET A. ASHLEY. [L. S.]

Sealed and delivered in ⎱
   the presence of   ⎰

EDWIN F. COREY, Ju'r, as to all.
JAMES P. SINNOTT, as to SAML. J. TILDEN.
G. BOTTA, as to O. D. ASHLEY and WIFE.

UNITED STATES OF AMERICA, ⎱
   State of New-York,   ⎰ ss.
City and County of New-York.

Be it known that on the sixth day of October, A. D. 1859, before me, the undersigned, Edwin F. Corey, Junior, resident in the City of New-York, and a commissioner duly commissioned and qualified by the executive authority, and under the laws of the State of Wisconsin, to take acknowledgment of deeds, &c., to be used or recorded therein, and a commissioner duly commissioned and qualified by the executive authority, and under the laws of the State of Michigan, to take the acknowledgment of deeds, &c., to be used or recorded therein, and a public notary in and for the State of New-York, by Letters Patent under the Great Seal of State, duly commissioned and sworn, personally appeared Samuel J. Tilden, Ossian D. Ashley and Harriet A. Ashley his wife, to me personally known to be the same persons described in and who executed the foregoing instrument of writing, and severally acknowledged that they signed, sealed and delivered the said instrument of writing as their free and voluntary act for the uses and purposes therein set forth; and the said Harriet A. Ashley, on a private examination by me made, separate and apart from her said husband, having had the contents of said instrument fully made known and explained to her by me, acknowledged that she executed the same, and relinquished her dower in the lands and tenements therein mentioned voluntarily and freely, and without any fear or compulsion of her said husband, and did not wish to retract the same.

In testimony whereof, I have hereunto set. my hand and affixed my seals of office, as such notary and commissioner, at my office in the City of New-York, the day and year first above written.

[L. S.] [L. S.]   Edwin F. Corey, Ju'r,

      [L. S.]   *Commissioner for Wisconsin and*
              Michigan, and Notary Public
                 in and for New-York.

THIS INDENTURE, made this first day of July, in the year of our Lord one thousand eight hundred and fifty-nine, between the CHICAGO AND NORTH WESTERN RAILWAY COMPANY, of the first part, and SAMUEL J. TILDEN, of the City and State of New-York, of the second part:

Whereas the said parties of the first part are a corporation, duly formed and organized in pursuance of a statute of the State of Wisconsin, entitled "An act to facilitate and authenticate the formation of a corporation, by the purchasers of the Chicago, St. Paul and Fond du Lac Rail-Road Company," approved March 14th, 1859, and of the laws of the State of Wisconsin ; and are likewise a corporation duly formed and organized in pursuance of a statute of the State of Illinois, entitled "An act to authorize the sale of the Chicago, St. Paul and Fond du Lac Rail-Road, and to enable the purchasers thereof to form a corporation," approved February 19th, 1859, and of the laws of the State of Illinois.

And whereas the said parties of the first part have become vested with the title to the rail-road formerly known as the Chicago, St. Paul and Fond du Lac Rail-Road, with its appurtenances, and of other property and franchises formerly owned or possessed by the Chicago, St. Paul and Fond du Lac Rail-Road Company, by deed bearing even date herewith, and made and delivered to the parties of the first part, by Samuel J. Tilden and Ossian D. Ashley, purchasers of the said rail-road property and franchises, in conformity to the aforesaid statutes and to the laws of the said States.

And whereas, for the purpose of completing and equipping the rail-road acquired as aforesaid, and now known as the Chicago and North Western Railway, and of funding debts which are liens upon certain of the aforesaid property, or have been assumed by the parties of the first part, as well as for the purpose of paying the consideration of the agreement between the said parties of the first part and the aforesaid purchasers, whereby the said railway and property were acquired, the said parties of the first part have resolved to make and deliver bonds of two classes, but secured by the same trust deed or mortgage, in the forms and amounts hereinafter specified.

The first class of the said bonds, designated as " sinking fund bonds," amount, in the aggregate, to one million and one hundred thousand dollars, with a contingent provision for a further issue of the additional amount of one hundred and fifty thousand dollars. They consist of two hundred and fifty of the denomination of one hundred dollars, and numbered consecutively from one to two hundred and fifty, inclusively ; two hundred and fifty of the denomination of two hundred dollars, and numbered consecutively from two hundred and fifty-one to five hundred, inclusively ; one hundred and fifty of the denomination of five hundred dollars, and numbered consecutively from five hundred and one to six hundred and fifty, inclusively ; and nine hundred and fifty of the denomination of one thousand dollars, and numbered consecutively from six hundred and fifty-one to sixteen hundred, inclusively; and the contingent issue of one hundred and-fifty of the denomination of one thousand dollars, and numbered consecutively from sixteen hundred and one to seventeen hundred and fifty, inclusively. All the bonds of the first class are dated the first day of July, one thousand eight hundred and fifty-nine ; are payable on the first day of August, A. D. one thousand eight hundred and eighty-five, at the office or agency of the parties of the first part, in the City of New-York ; bear interest from the first day of August, A. D. one thousand eight hundred and fifty-nine, at the rate of seven per centum per annum, payable semi-annually at the said office or agency, on the first days of February and August in each year; are equally and ratably secured by this instrument, and, according to their respective amounts, entitled to the advantages of the special preferred lien herein established in their favor, and the benefits to be derived from the sinking fund herein provided ; and are in the form following :

No.   UNITED STATES OF AMERICA. $——

STATES OF ILLINOIS AND WISCONSIN.

CHICAGO AND NORTH WESTERN RAILWAY COMPANY.

FIRST MORTGAGE SINKING FUND BOND.

KNOW ALL MEN BY THESE PRESENTS, that the Chicago and North Western Railway Company are indebted to Samuel

J. Tilden, of the City of New-York, or bearer, in the sum of
dollars, lawful money of the United States
of America, which the said company promise and agree to
pay to the said Samuel J. Tilden, or bearer hereof, on the
first day of August, A. D. 1885, at the office or agency of
the said company, in the City of New-York, with interest
thereon from the first day of August, 1859, at the rate of
seven per centum per annum, payable semi-annually by the
said company, at their office or agency in the City of New-
York, on the first days of February and August in each year,
on the presentation and surrender of the annexed coupons as
they severally become due ; and in case of non-payment of
interest for any half year, if demanded, and the same remaining in arrear for six months thereafter, the principal
shall become due and payable as provided in the trust deed
hereinafter mentioned.

This bond is one of a series of bonds of the same tenor and
date, but of several denominations, which bonds amount, in
the aggregate, to one million and one hundred thousand dollars, with contingent provision for a further issue of an amount
not exceeding one hundred and fifty thousand dollars, and
form the first class of bonds, the payment of which is secured
by a deed of trust duly executed and delivered by the said
railway company to Samuel J. Tilden, trustee, and conveying
the railway of the said company from Chicago to a point
twenty miles northerly from Fond du Lac, and all the depot
grounds, depots, equipments and other things pertaining thereto, and all the franchises of the said company, as by reference
to said trust deed, bearing date on the first day of July, A.
D. 1859, and duly recorded, will more fully appear. And
the holder hereof is entitled to the priorities established in
favor of the said first class of bonds by the said deed of trust,
and to the advantage of the special preferred lien created by
the said deed of trust upon all the property and things therein
embraced ; the holder hereof is also entitled to the benefits
which may be derived from a sinking fund to be set apart
annually by the said company, as specified and provided for
in said deed of trust.

This bond entitles the person registered on the books of the
company as the holder thereof, at the time of any general or
special meeting of the stockholders, to one vote for every one
hundred dollars of the par amount thereof, as a special stock
created under the act of the State of Wisconsin, approved
March 14th, 1859, and the laws of that State and of Illinois,

but such stock is not subject to assessment nor entitled to dividends.

This bond shall not be valid or obligatory until it shall have been authenticated by a certificate endorsed thereon, and duly signed by the said trustee or his successor.

This bond may pass by delivery, or it may be registered on the books of the company, at the option of any holder; and after such registration and the endorsement of a certificate thereof upon the bond, no transfer shall be valid unless such transfer be registered and endorsed as aforesaid, or unless the last registry be to bearer or in blank.

IN WITNESS WHEREOF, the said company have caused their corporate seal to be hereto affixed, and their president and treasurer to sign, and their secretary to countersign the same, and have also caused the coupons hereto annexed to be signed by their assistant secretary, this first day of July, in the year of our Lord one thousand eight hundred and fifty-nine.

President.

Treasurer.

Countersigned by

Secretary.

The second class of the said bonds, amounting, in the aggregate, to three millions and five hundred thousand dollars, with a contingent provision for a further issue to the additional amount of one hundred thousand dollars, consist of two hundred and fifty of the denomination of one hundred dollars, and numbered consecutively from seventeen hundred and fifty-one to two thousand, inclusively; two hundred and fifty of the denomination of two hundred dollars, and numbered consecutively from two thousand and one to two thousand two hundred and fifty, inclusively; two hundred and fifty of the denomination of five hundred dollars, and numbered consecutively from two thousand two hundred and fifty-one to two thousand five hundred, inclusively; and thirty-three hundred of the denomination of one thousand dollars, numbered consecutively from two thousand five hundred and one to five thousand eight hundred, inclusively, and the contingent issue of one hundred of the like denomination, numbered consecutively from five thousand eight hundred and one to five thousand nine hundred, inclusively. All the bonds of the second class are dated the first day of July, 1859, and are payable on the first day of August, 1885, at the office or agency of the parties of the first part, in the City of New-

York; bear interest from the first day of August, A. D. 1860, at the rate of seven per centum per annum, payable semi-annually at the said office or agency, on the first days of February and August in each year, and are equally and ratably secured by this instrument, according to their respective amounts, and are in the form following:

UNITED STATES OF AMERICA.

No. STATES OF ILLINOIS AND WISCONSIN. $——

CHICAGO AND NORTH WESTERN RAILWAY COMPANY.

FIRST MORTGAGE BOND.

KNOW ALL MEN BY THESE PRESENTS, that the Chicago and North Western Railway Company are indebted to Samuel J. Tilden, of the City of New-York, or bearer, in the sum of —— dollars, lawful money of the United States of America, which the said company promise and agree to pay to the said Samuel J. Tilden, or bearer hereof, on the first day of August, A. D. 1885, at the office or agency of the said company, in the City of New-York, with interest thereon from the first day of August, 1860, at the rate of seven per centum per annum, payable semi-annually by the said company, at their office or agency in the City of New-York, on the first days of February and August in each year, on the presentation and surrender of the annexed coupons as they severally become due. And in case of the non-payment of interest for any half year, if demanded, and the same remaining in arrear for six months thereafter, the principal shall become due and payable as provided in the trust deed hereinafter mentioned.

This bond is one of a series of bonds of the same tenor and date, but of several denominations, which bonds amount, in the aggregate, to three millions and five hundred thousand dollars, with contingent provision for a further issue to an amount not exceeding one hundred thousand dollars; and which, with an issue of preferred sinking fund bonds secured by the same trust deed, amount in the aggregate to four millions six hundred thousand dollars; with contingent provision for a further issue to an amount not exceeding two hundred and fifty thousand dollars, the payment of all of which is secured by a deed of trust duly executed and delivered by the said railway company to Samuel J. Tilden, trustee, and conveying the railway of the said company from

Chicago to a point twenty miles northerly from Fond du Lac, and all the depot grounds, depots, equipments and other things pertaining thereto ; and all the franchises of the said company, subject to the priorities in the said trust deed provided in favor of the issues of preferred sinking fund bonds therein mentioned, as by reference to the said trust deed, bearing date on the first day of July, A. D. 1859, and duly recorded, will more fully appear.

This bond entitles the person registered on the books of the company, as the holder thereof, at the time of any general or special meeting of the stockholders, to one vote for every one hundred dollars of the par amount thereof, as a special stock created under the act of the State of Wisconsin, approved March 14th, 1859, and the laws of that State and of Illinois ; but such stock is not subject to assessment nor entitled to dividends.

This bond shall not be valid or obligatory until it shall have been authenticated by a certificate endorsed hereon, and duly signed by the said trustee or his successor.

This bond may pass by delivery, or it may be registered on the books of the company at the option of any holder; and after such registration, and the endorsement of a certificate thereof upon the bond, no transfer shall be valid, unless such transfer be registered and endorsed as aforesaid, or unless the last registry be to bearer or in blank.

IN WITNESS WHEREOF, the said company have caused their corporate seal to be hereto affixed, and their president and treasurer to sign, and their secretary to countersign the same, and have also caused the coupons hereto annexed to be signed by their assistant secretary, this first day of July, in the year of our Lord one thousand eight hundred and fifty-nine.

President.

Treasurer.

Countersigned by

Secretary.

Of the contingent issues herein provided for, one hundred thousand dollars of the first class of bonds is for new and additional equipment, engine and car-houses and other construction, as well for the old as for the new portions of the said railway, as may be from time to time required by its business ; and the remaining fifty thousand dollars of bonds of the first class, and the one hundred thousand dollars of bonds of the second class, are to be applied as aforesaid, or if needful, to the liquidating of specific liens upon portions of the property acquired as aforesaid, and funding the bonded debts assumed by the parties of the first part. All of which bonds, so issued or to be issued, are hereby declared and agreed to be given as consideration for the purchase of the said railway, property, rights and franchises as hereinbefore recited.

NOW THIS INDENTURE witnesseth, that the parties of the first part, in consideration of the premises, and of one dollar to them in hand paid, the receipt whereof is hereby acknowledged, and in order to secure the payment of the principal and interest of the bonds aforesaid, issued or to be issued as herein recited and provided, and every part of the said principal and interest, as the same shall become payable, according to the tenor of the said bonds, and of the coupons thereto annexed, have granted, bargained, sold, conveyed and transferred, and do, by these presents, grant, bargain, sell, convey and transfer unto the party of the second part, and his heirs and assigns, and unto the successors of the said party of the second part in the trust hereinafter created and set forth, and the respective heirs and assigns of such successors, all the railway of the parties of the first part, extending from the City of Chicago, in the State of Illinois, to a point twenty miles northerly from the City of Fond du Lac, and about four miles northerly from the City of Oshkosh, in the State of Wisconsin, by way of the cities of Janesville, Fond du Lac and Oshkosh, in the said State, and including that portion of the said railway between the said cities of Janesville and the La Crosse or Minnesota Junction, which is now in process of construction, as the same shall be hereafter finished, as fully and effectually as if the whole of the said railway were completed before the execution of these presents; including all the railways, ways and rights of way, depot grounds and other lands; all tracks, bridges, viaducts, culverts, fences and other structures; all depots, station houses, engine houses, car houses, freight houses, wood houses and other buildings; and all machine shops and other shops; whether now held or hereafter acquired for use, in connection with the said railway or the business thereof; and including, also, all locomotives, tenders, cars and other rolling stock or equipment, and all machinery, tools, implements, fuel and materials for the constructing, operating, repairing or replacing the said railway, or any part thereof, or any of its equipment or appurtenances, whether now held or hereafter acquired; all of which things are hereby declared to be appurtenances and fixtures of the said railway; and also all franchises connected with or relating to the said railway, or the construction, maintenance or use thereof, now held or hereafter acquired by the said parties of the first part; and all corporate and other franchises which are now or may be hereafter possessed or exercised by the said parties of the first part:

Together with all and singular the tenements, hereditaments and appurtenances thereunto belonging or in any wise appertaining, and the reversions, remainders, tolls, incomes, rents, issues and profits thereof; and also all the estate, right, title, interest, property, possession, claim and demand whatsoever, as well in law as in equity, of the said parties of the first part, of, in and to the same, and any and every part thereof, with the appurtenances; *reserving*, nevertheless, to the said parties of the first part full power, with the approval in writing of the trustee herein provided, for the time being, to sell or exchange any lands which may be held for the use of any of the aforesaid depots, shops or other buildings, or for a supply of fuel or gravel, or other material, for which purpose full power is hereby conferred on the said trustee to release any lands so sold or exchanged from the lien of these presents; but the lands acquired in substitution for any so sold or exchanged, shall become subject to the operation of these presents, with the same effect as if originally embraced herein by specific description; and every surplus of money or assets which may arise from any such sale or exchange, shall be subject to the control and custody of the said trustee, or invested with his approval; *reserving*, also, to the parties of the first part, for the purpose of erecting, or causing or procuring to be erected, for the use of the said railway, or for use in connection therewith, grain or freight or other warehouses or depot buildings, full power, with the approval of the trustee for the time being, to convey, sell, lease or mortgage such portions of the said lands as may be occupied or required to be occupied by, or necessarily used or needed for, any warehouse or warehouses, or other depot buildings, which may be erected as aforesaid; for which purpose full power is hereby granted to the trustee for the time being to release such portions of the said lands from the lien of these presents; and *reserving*, also, to the said parties of the first part full power, from time to time to dispose of, according to their discretion, such portions of the said equipment, machinery and implements as may have become unfit or unnecessary for the use of the said parties of the first part, and to replace the same by new, which shall thereupon become subject to the operation of these presents as aforesaid ; and *reserving*, also, to the said parties of the first part full power to withdraw from the operation of these presents the portion of the aforesaid railway which is situate northerly from the Wolf River, at the City of Oshkosh, for the purpose of encouraging the extension of the said railway from the said City of Oshkosh to Appleton ; for which purpose full power is hereby conferred on the said trustee to release the said portion from the lien of these presents : and *subject*, nevertheless, in respect to certain of the aforesaid lands situate in the City of Chicago, and acquired for depot grounds, which are described in a trust deed of William B. Ogden to Azariah C. Flagg, bearing date the first day of January, one thousand eight hundred and fifty-seven, and recorded in the office of the Recorder of Cook County, in the State of Illinois, on the twenty-third day of February, one thousand eight hundred and fifty-seven, in book one hundred and twenty-one of deeds, page three hundred and sixty four, and to the provisions of the said trust deed and the prior lien created thereby ; and in respect to certain other of the aforesaid lands, also situate and acquired as aforesaid, which are described in a trust deed of the said William B. Ogden to Richard H. Winslow, bearing date on the thirty-first day of May, one thousand eight hundred and fifty-eight, and recorded in the office of the said Recorder on the seventh day of August, one thousand eight hundred and fifty-eight, in book one hundred and fifty-six of deeds, page six hundred and twenty-five, and to the provisions of the said last mentioned trust deed, and the prior lien created thereby ; the obligations secured by which said incumbrances, the parties of the first part have assumed and agreed to pay, and in evidence and security thereof, have executed and delivered a trust deed of the aforesaid lands to the said Azariah C. Flagg, bearing even date herewith, but to which, as respects the aforesaid lands, these presents are subject :

To have and to hold the above described premises and appurtenances, but subject to the reservations, conditions and provisions herein contained, unto the said party of the second part, and his heirs and assigns, and unto the several successors of the said party of the second part, in the trust hereby created, and their respective heirs and assigns, to the only proper use and behoof of the said party and his heirs and assigns, and of the said successors and their respective heirs and assigns, in trust, nevertheless, for the following purposes, to wit :

1. In case default shall be made by the parties of the first part, or their successors or assigns, in the payment of any interest on any of the aforesaid bonds, according to the tenor of the coupons thereto annexed, or in the payment of any principal of any of such bonds, as the same shall become demandable, or in any payment required by these presents to be made into the sinking fund herein provided, or in any covenant or agreement of the said parties of the first part, herein required to be performed or kept by the said parties; and if such default shall continue for the period of three months, it shall be lawful for the said trustee himself, or by his attorneys or agents, to enter into and upon all and singular the premises hereby conveyed, or intended so to be, and each and every part thereof; and himself, or by his attorneys or agents, to have, hold, use and enjoy the same; himself, or by his superintendents, managers, receivers or servants operating the said railway, and conducting the business thereof, and making, from time to time, all repairs and replacements, and all useful alterations, additions and improvements thereto, as fully as the parties of the first part might have done before such entry; and to collect and receive all tolls, freights, incomes, rents, issues and profits of the same, and of every part thereof; and after deducting the expenses of operating the said railway and conducting its business, and of all the said repairs, replacements, alterations, additions and improvements, and all payments for taxes, assessments, charges or liens on the said premises, or on any part thereof, and as well as just compensation for his own services, to apply the residue of the moneys arising as aforesaid:

First.—To the payment of the interest on such of the aforesaid bonds as are herein designated as sinking fund bonds, in the order in which such interest shall have become due, or shall become due, and to the persons holding the coupons evidencing the right to such interest.

Secondly.—After paying all the aforesaid interest then due, and making such provision as to the said trustee may seem advisable for any half-year's interest next to fall due, to the payment of the interest on the others of the aforesaid bonds not herein designated as sinking fund bonds, in the order aforesaid, and to the persons holding the coupons evidencing the right to such interest.

Thirdly.—To the payments required by these presents to be made into the sinking fund hereby provided.

And if at any time the moneys applicable to any class of the said payments shall not suffice to pay the said class in full, the said moneys shall be applied ratably towards such payments. And in case all the said payments, of every class, shall have been made in full, and no sale shall have been made in conformity hereto, the said trustee shall restore the possession of the premises hereby conveyed unto the said party of the first part, its successors or assigns; provided, that if any of the defaults hereinbefore specified be subsequently made, such restoration shall not, nor shall any previous entry, be construed to exhaust or in any manner impair the powers of entry or sale, or any powers hereby granted to or conferred upon the said trustee.

2. In case default shall be made as aforesaid, and shall continue as aforesaid, it shall likewise be lawful for the said trustee, after entry as aforesaid, or other entry, or without entry, himself or by his attorneys or agents, to sell and dispose of all and singular the premises hereby conveyed, or intended so to be, or any portion thereof, and all right, benefit and equity of redemption of the parties of the first part, their successors and assigns, at public auction, in the City of New-York, or in the City of Chicago, or in such other place in the State of Wisconsin as the said trustee or his attorneys or agents may designate, or in any one or more of those places, and at such time or times as he or they may appoint, having first given notice of the place or places, and the time or times of such sale or sales, by advertisement published not less than three times a week for six weeks in one or more newspapers in each of said cities of New-York and Chicago, or to adjourn the said sale or sales from time to time, in his or their discretion; and, if so adjourning, to make the same at the time or times, and place or places, to which the same may be so adjourned; and to sell, subject to the lien created by these presents in favor of such of the aforesaid bonds as are herein designated as sinking fund bonds, or discharged of such lien; and, if selling in the first instance subject to such lien, then to retain, hold and exercise the powers of entry, sale and conveyance, and all the powers conferred by these presents, as amply as if they had not been once exercised; and, as the attorney in fact of the said parties of the first part, their successors or assigns, for such purpose duly and irrevocably constituted, or in the name of the said trustee, to make and deliver to the purchaser or purchasers thereof, good and sufficient deed or deeds in the law for the same in fee simple; and to make the said deed or deeds subject to the said lien or otherwise; which sale or sales made as aforesaid, and whether subject to the said lien

or otherwise, shall be a perpetual bar both in law and equity, against the said parties of the first part, their successors and assigns, and all other persons claiming or to claim the said premises, or any part thereof, by, from or under them, or any of them; and to apply the proceeds of such sale or sales, after deducting just allowances for all expenses of the said sale or sales, including attorneys' and counsel fees and all other expenses, advances and liabilities, which may have been made or incurred by the said trustee in the operating or maintaining the said railway or managing of its business, and all payments for taxes, assessments, charges or liens on the said premises, or any part thereof, or in administering the said trust, as well as compensation for his own services, and paying the lien created by the aforesaid trust deed of said parties of the first part to the said A. C. Flagg, in the manner following:

If the said sale or sales shall have been made, subject to the lien created by these presents, in favor of such of the aforesaid bonds as are herein designated as sinking fund bonds, then the said trustee shall apply the said net proceeds, *first*, to the payment of the interest then due on the said sinking fund bonds in the order in which the said interest shall have become due, and to the persons holding the coupons evidencing the right to such interest; and after paying in full all such interest, then to any payments which ought at that time to be made, according to the requirements of these presents, into the sinking fund herein provided; and if any half-year's interest on the said sinking fund bonds shall at that time have partially accrued, retaining and reserving, in the discretion of the said trustee, from such proceeds, the means to pay such half-year's interest at maturity; *secondly*, after paying and retaining as aforesaid, to the payment of the interest then due on those of the said bonds, not herein designated as sinking fund bonds, in the order aforesaid, to the persons holding the coupons evidencing the right to such interest; and after paying in full all such interest to the payment of the principal of those of the said bonds, not herein designated as sinking fund bonds, whether such principal be then due or not; and in case the portion of the said proceeds which may be applicable to either of the aforesaid classes of payments shall not be sufficient to make the payment of such class in full, the said portion shall be applied ratably towards the said payments. But, if the said sale or sales shall have been made, in the first instance, so as to discharge the prior lien created by these presents in favor of such of the aforesaid

bonds as are herein designated as sinking fund bonds ; or if
any sale or sales of the said premises shall at any time be made
so as to discharge the aforesaid lien, then, and in either of such
cases, the said trustee, after deducting just allowances, and
paying, as hereinbefore more fully specified for the case of
sale, shall apply the net proceeds of such sale or sales, in the
manner following: *first*, to the payment of the interest
then due on such of the aforesaid bonds as are herein
designated as sinking fund bonds, in the order in which said
interest shall have become due, and to the persons holding
the coupons evidencing the right to such interest, and next to
the payment of the principal of the said sinking fund bonds,
whether such principal be then due or not; and the
residue, after making the said payments in full, and after
refunding, with interest at seven per cent., any advances
to pay interest on the said sinking fund bonds, which may
have been made or procured to be made in pursuance of any
resolution or authority of holders of a majority in amount of
the second class of the bonds, to the payment of the interest
then due on such of the aforesaid bonds as are not herein
designated as sinking fund bonds in the order in which such
interest shall have become due, and to the persons holding
the coupons, evidencing the right to such interest ; and next
thereafter to the payment of the principal of the said last
mentioned bonds, whether such principal be then due or not;
and in case the portion of the said proceeds which may be
applicable, according to the aforesaid order of priority, to any
of the aforesaid classes of payments, shall not suffice to make
the payments of such class in full, the said portion shall be
applied ratably towards the said payments.

And it is hereby declared, that the receipt or receipts of
the said trustee shall be a sufficient discharge to the purchaser or purchasers of the premises, or any part thereof, for
his or their purchase money ; and that such purchaser or
purchasers, his or their heirs, executors or administrators,
shall not, after payment thereof, and having such receipt, be
liable to see to its being applied upon or for the trusts and
purposes of these presents, or in any manner howsoever be
answerable for any loss, misapplication or non-application of
such purchase money, or any part thereof, or be obliged to
inquire into the necessity, expediency or authority of or for
any such sale or sales.

Provided, always, and the grant and conveyance herein
contained are upon the express condition that if the said
parties of the first part shall well and truly pay, or cause to be

paid, the interest on the said bonds, so issued or to be issued as aforesaid, as the same shall fall due and be demanded, and also the principal thereof, when the same shall fall due, or shall exhibit the said bonds, cancelled, to the said party of the second part, or his successor in the said trust, then the estate, title and interest of the party of the second part, and his successors in the trust, shall cease, determine and become void; but otherwise they shall remain in full force and virtue.

And the said parties of the first part hereby covenant and agree to and with the said party of the second part and his successors, that in case default shall be made by the said parties of the first part, or their successors or assigns, in the payment of any half-year's interest, on any of the bouds herein designated as sinking fund bonds, at the time and in the manner in the coupon issued therewith provided, the said coupon having been presented, and the payment of the interest therein specified been demanded; and in case such default shall continue for the period of six months after the said coupon shall have become due, then and in that case the principal of the bonds in respect to which such default shall have happened shall become, and at the election of the said trustee, to be made at any time without notice, the principal of all the said bonds of both classes shall become due and payable, any thing therein contained to the contrary notwithstanding; and in case default shall be made and continue as aforesaid, in the payment of any half-year's interest on any of the aforesaid bonds of the second class, then, and in that case, the principal of the bonds in respect to which such default shall have happened shall become, and at the election of the said trustee, to be made at any time without notice, the principal of all of the said bonds of the second class shall become due and payable, any thing therein contained to the contrary notwithstanding; *provided*, *nevertheless*, that the operation of this provision may be suspended in the cases and in the manner hereinafter expressed.

And the said parties of the first part hereby further covenant and agree to and with the said party of the second part and his successors, that for the further security and ultimate redemption of such of the aforesaid bonds as are herein designated as sinking fund bonds, the said parties of the first part, their successors or assigns, will, on or before the first day of December, in each and every year, until the principal of the said bonds shall be wholly paid, beginning on the first day of December, in the year one thousand eight hundred and sixty-four, set apart and appropriate, out of the earnings of the said railway for the preceding year, and will, on or before the said day, deposit with, and pay to the trustee, for the time being, the full sum of twenty-five thousand dollars; which sum, together with all accumulations of interest thereon that may actually come into the hands of the said trustee, shall be laid out and invested by the said trustee in the purchase of bonds, herein designated as aforesaid, provided the same can be purchased at a rate not exceeding the par of said bonds, and interest; and the bonds so purchased shall be held by the said trustee, and immediately stamped or endorsed as belonging to the said sinking fund, but shall continue in force, and the interest thereon shall continue to be paid by the parties of the first part, and the amount thereof shall be added to and applied as a part of the capital of the sinking fund hereby established, and be laid out and invested in the manner and within the limitation, as herein provided.

And preparatory to the purchase of bonds as aforesaid, the said trustee shall give thirty days' notice thereof, in two or more of the daily newspapers published in the city of New-York, and shall make the said purchase at the lowest price or prices at which the same may be offered in pursuance of such notice, or at such lower price or prices as he may be able to obtain the same, but not exceeding the par and interest of said bonds; and in case the said bonds cannot be purchased at par and interest, as above, within three months after the expiration of the notice aforesaid, then the said trustee may, in his discretion, invest the said sinking fund moneys in the purchase of the bonds of the second class, at the lowest prices, not exceeding par and interest, at which they may be obtained, after notice as aforesaid.

And the said trustee shall furnish an annual statement or exhibit, to be submitted to the stockholders at their annual meeting, of the number and denomination of the bonds so purchased by him for the sinking fund; which bonds he shall also cause to be transferred and registered on the Bond Register, kept in the office or agency of the parties of the first part, in the City of New-York, in the name of "The Trustee of the Sinking Fund;" so that the said Register will, at all times, show what bonds belong to said sinking fund; and the said trustee may vote on such bonds. And the said trustee shall and will at all times, on reasonable notice and request, furnish to the party of the first part a particular statement or account, exhibiting the condition of the said sinking fund.

And the said parties of the first part hereby agree with the said party of the second part, and his successors, that the said parties of the first part will not at any time hereafter use or appropriate any of the proper earnings of the railway hereby conveyed, or incur any debt or liability for any purpose other than the completing, equipping, operating, repairing or replacing of the said railway or its appurtenances, providing facilities for its business, paying liens on its property, or carrying on its proper transactions, unless with the consent, in writing, of the holders of a majority in amount of each class of the aforesaid bonds, first had and obtained, or by resolutions at meetings duly held of the said two classes.

And the said parties of the first part hereby further covenant and agree to and with the said party of the second part, and his successors, that a book shall, at all times hereafter, be kept by the parties of the first part and their successors, at their office or agency in the City of New-York, which shall be designated as the Voting Register of the First Mortgage Bondholders, and shall be distinct from the Transfer Register of the bonds; that the registry therein contained of the two classes of bonds secured by these presents shall be kept separately; that any holder of any of the said bonds shall be entitled to have his name and address, and the class and denomination of every of the said bonds held by him, entered in such registry on presenting, at the aforesaid office or agency, a written statement of the said particulars, signed by himself; and, if required, duly verifying his title thereto by producing the bonds, or in such other mode as may be prescribed by the regulations for such verification; that the parties of the first part may, in the first instance, prescribe the said regulations, subject to the power hereby declared of the bondholders of each class, acting by a majority in interest, to adopt, alter or repeal, from time to time, the said regulations, and generally to establish such as seem to them expedient; that such registration shall authenticate the right of the holder of every bond so registered to vote on the said bond, as provided therein, at every general and special meeting of the stockholders of the said parties of the first part; and shall also entitle the said holder to notice, in such mode and form as may be fixed by regulations prescribed or established as aforesaid, of all meetings of his class of the first mortgage bondholders; that the trustee for the time being shall at all times have free access to such book of registry, and shall, from time to time, and at all times, on his request in writing, be furnished with a copy thereof by the parties of the first part; but, nevertheless, shall have a right to require, at his option, that any act or resolution of the said bondholders of either class affecting his duties or the interest of the trust hereby created, shall be authenticated by the signatures of all the persons assenting thereto, as well as by a minute of the proceedings of the meeting ; that meetings of either or both of the said classes of the first mortgage bondholders may be called by the trustee for the time being, or in such other mode as may be fixed by regulations prescribed or established as aforesaid, and the bondholders may vote thereat in person or by proxy ; and that such other regulations or by-laws in respect to such meetings may be from time to time made and established by the bondholders of each class, acting by a majority in interest, as to them shall seem expedient.

And the parties of the first part hereby covenant to and with the party of the second part and his several successors in the trust hereby created, and his and their respective assigns, that the parties of the first part, and their successors and assigns, shall and will, from time to time, and at all times hereafter, execute, deliver and acknowledge all and every such further deeds, conveyances and assurances in the law for the better assuring unto the party of the second part and his several successors in the trust hereby created, and his and their respective heirs and assigns, of the premises in manner as above conveyed or expressed, or intended to be conveyed, as well in reference to property or things at any time or times hereafter acquired, as to such as are now owned or possessed by the parties of the first part, or for the better effectuating of the intent and objects of these presents, as by the said party of the second part, or his several successors in the trust hereby created, or his or their respective assigns, or his or their counsel learned in the law, shall be reasonably advised, devised or required : And that the above described premises, and every part thereof, in the quiet and peaceable possession of the said party of the second part, and his several successors in the trust hereby created, and his and their respective heirs and assigns, against all and every person or persons lawfully claiming, or to claim the whole, or any part thereof, the said parties of the first part shall and will warrant and forever defend.

It is mutually agreed, by and between the parties hereto, that it shall be the duty of the trustee for the time being to exercise the power of entry, or the power of sale hereby granted, or both, upon the requisition, in writing, as hereinafter specified as applicable to the several cases of default, subject to the qualifications hereinafter expressed, in the manner hereinafter provided, as follows:

1. If the default be as to the interest or principal of the sinking fund bonds, the requisition shall be by holders of one hundred thousand dollars of the sinking fund bonds, or holders of one million dollars of bonds of the second class ; but, in both such cases, holders of a majority in amount of the sinking fund bonds may instruct the trustee to defer the entry for periods which shall not exceed six months at any one time, or one year in all from the accrual of the right of entry, and may instruct the said trustee to defer the exercise of the power of sale for like periods ; and the said majority may also, for the period for which such entry or sale shall be deferred, suspend the provision of the said sinking fund bonds, whereby, on default in respect to interest, as in the said bonds specified, the principal thereof would become due.

2. If the default be as to interest or principal of bonds of the second class, the requisition shall be by holders of three hundred thousand dollars of such bonds ; but holders of a majority in amount of the bonds of the second class may instruct the trustee to defer the entry or the exercise of the power of sale, from time to time, in their discretion, but for periods not exceeding one year at any one time ; and the said majority may also, in like manner, suspend the provision of the bonds of the second class, whereby, on default in respect to interest, as in the said bonds specified, the principal thereof would become due, whether such default be in respect to interest on either the first or second class of the said bonds.

3. If the default be as to any payment into the sinking fund herein provided for bonds of the first class, the requisition shall be by holders of a majority in amount of such bonds ; but such holders may instruct the trustee to defer or omit the entry and the exercise of the power of sale according to their discretion ; and whether so instructed or not, the trustee, if he shall be satisfied that the said railway, being well managed, and its net earnings fairly applied, first to the payment of interest on the sinking fund bonds, and next to the payment of interest on the bonds of the second class, nevertheless fails to afford a surplus over such payments sufficient to make good the sinking fund, as herein provided, may, in his discretion, defer or omit the exercise of the powers of entry and sale.

4. If the default be as to any of the covenants, other than those above specified, the requisition shall be by holders of a

majority in amount of the sinking fund bonds, or a majority in amount of the bonds of the second class ; but holders of a majority in amount of both classes united may instruct the trustee to defer or omit the exercise of the powers of entry and sale, according to their discretion.

5. If the default be as to interest on the bonds of the second class, but there be no default in respect to interest or principal of the sinking fund bonds, or in payments into the sinking fund, then and in that case—or if at any time, not less than thirty days before the time or times notified for a sale or sales of the premises hereby conveyed, by reason of default in respect to the sinking fund bonds, the payments so in default in respect to the sinking fund bonds shall be advanced or paid to the trustee, under the authority or with the sanction of holders of a majority in amount of the bonds of the second class, or of a resolution adopted at a meeting duly held of such bondholders, then and in either of such cases the sale or sales of the premises aforesaid shall be made subject to the prior lien created by these presents in favor of the sinking fund bonds ; and if the sale or sales be made subject as aforesaid, and if a default in the payment of interest on the said sinking fund bonds shall have happened, whereby the principal thereof would become due, the said provision shall be suspended by the trustee until another default shall happen.

Provided, nevertheless, that the aforesaid provisions regulating the discretion of the trustee in the exercise of the aforesaid powers granted by these presents, or either of them, shall operate for such purpose only as between the trustee and the bondholders ; and shall not, nor shall any of the said provisions, avail or be construed to operate as conditions to the valid or effectual exercise of the said powers, or either of them, or to defeat or affect any entry, sale or conveyance which he may make by virtue of the powers of entry or sale granted by these presents.

And it is mutually agreed by and between the parties hereto, as a condition on which the party of the second part has assented to these presents, that until a default and requisition, as hereinbefore defined and provided, the trustee for the time being shall not be required to perform any active duty ; that the said trustee may at all times and in all cases act in the said trust by one or more of such attorneys, agents and servants as he may from time to time appoint or constitute, as validly and effectually in all respects as if acting personally ; that the said trustee shall not be, in any manner, responsible for any default or misconduct of any such attorney, agent or servant whom he may at any time so appoint or constitute, or for any thing other than his own wilful default or misconduct; that the said trustee shall be entitled to just compensation for all services which he may hereafter render in his trust; that a resolution, adopted by a majority in interest of either class of the said bondholders, requesting, approving or ratifying any act or omission on the part of the said trustee, shall be full and conclusive justification of him as against each and all of the holders of the bonds of the said class, and shall acquit and discharge him from all accountability to such holders for and in respect to such act or omission; but this provision shall not be construed to authorize any deviation from the rule established by these presents for the distribution of net earnings or proceeds of the said railway and property among the bondholders of the said class, according to the proportions of their respective interests; that the said trustee may resign and discharge himself of the trust created by these presents by notice in writing to the parties of the first part, or their successors or assigns, and also to the immediate successor of the said trustee, if such successor shall have been designated herein, or in conformity to the provisions herein contained; that the said trustee may be removed by the vote of a majority in interest of the holders of the aforesaid bonds of the first class and a vote of a majority in interest of the holders of the aforesaid bonds of the second class; the said votes concurring and being had at meetings duly held of the said bondholders, and attested by an instrument under the hands and seals of the persons so voting, and acknowledged in the manner required in the States of Wisconsin and Illinois in order to entitle a conveyance to be recorded; that in case the party of the second part shall die, resign or be removed, his immediate successor shall be William Allen Butler, of the City of New-York; and in case the said William Allen Butler shall die, resign or be removed, or shall disclaim or decline to act, the second successor of the said trustee shall be William T. Booth, of the said city; that the trustee for the time being shall have power, with the consent of the holders of a majority in amount of each class of the said bonds, if concurring, to remove any immediate or other successor who may have been designated, and shall have power, with the like consent, if the majorities of such classes concur, but if they differ, in his own discretion to appoint an immediate or a second successor, in case either shall have died, resigned or been removed, or shall have disclaimed or declined, or become incapable or unfit to act; and shall have power, with the consent of holders of a majority in amount of both classes of the said bonds, to appoint not exceeding two new trustees to be associated with himself in the trust; that in case at any time hereafter any trustee shall die or resign or be removed, as herein provided, or by a court of competent jurisdiction, or in case any trustee shall become incapable or unfit to act in the said trust, and no successor shall have been provided in conformity hereto, a new trustee or new trustees, not exceeding three in number, may be appointed by the holders of a majority in amount of the first class of the said bonds; that the word trustee, as used in these presents, shall be construed to mean the trustee who may be at the time acting, or, if the number be increased, the trustees who may be at the time acting; that upon the accession or appointment of any new trustee or trustees, he or they shall become vested with all the powers and authorities and estates granted to or conferred upon the trustee or the party of the second part by these presents, and all the rights and interests requisite to enable the person or persons so acceding or appointed to execute the purposes of this trust, without any further assurance or conveyance; but all conveyances and other instruments shall be from time to time executed by the said trustee, and by the parties of the first part, which the counsel of the said trustee shall reasonably devise or advise for the purpose of assuring the legal estate in the premises to the trustee or trustees, who shall for the time being be designated as successors in the said trust, or appointed as trustee or trustees; and upon the death, resignation or removal of any trustee, or an appointment in his place, in pursuance of these presents, all his powers and authorities by virtue hereof shall cease; and if and as soon as effectual provision shall have been made for vesting the legal estate in the said premises in his successor or successors, all the estate, right, title and interest of the said trustee so dying, resigning or being removed, in the said premises, shall be divested and wholly cease and determine.

And it is hereby agreed, between the parties to this Indenture, that in the mean time, and until default shall be made in the payment of the interest or principal of the said bonds, or of some of them, or some part thereof, or in the payments into the sinking fund, or in some of the covenants or agreements herein contained, to be kept by the said parties of the first part, it shall be lawful for the said parties of the first part and their successors, peaceably and quietly to have,

hold, use, possess and enjoy the said premises, with the appurtenances, and to receive the incomes, tolls, rents, issues
and profits thereof, to their own use and benefit, without
any hindrance or interruption, suit or disturbance whatsoever of or by the said party of the second part, or his
successors in the trust, or any other person whatever, lawfully
claiming or to claim the same by, from or under him or them,
or any of them.

IN TESTIMONY WHEREOF, the said parties of the first part have
caused their corporate seal to be affixed to these presents, and
the same to be attested by the signatures of their President
and Treasurer, and the said party of the second part has
hereunto set his hand and seal, to testify his acceptance of
the said trust, the day and year first above written.

W. B. OGDEN, President.

[L. S.]   E. W. HUTCHINGS, *Treasurer.*

SAMUEL J. TILDEN. [L. S.]

Signed, sealed and delivered in the }
    presence of }

H. H. BOODY,
EDWIN F. COREY, JU'R.

UNITED STATES OF AMERICA, } ss.
STATE OF NEW-YORK, CITY AND COUNTY OF NEW-YORK,

Be it known, that on the seventh day of October, in
the year one thousand eight hundred and fifty-nine, before
me, the undersigned, Edwin F. Corey, Junior, resident in the
City of New-York, and a commissioner, duly commissioned
and qualified by the executive authority and under the laws
of the State of Wisconsin, to take acknowledgment of deeds,
&c., to be used or recorded therein, and a public notary in
and for the State of New-York, by Letters Patent under the
Great Seal of State, duly commissioned and sworn, personally
appeared WILLIAM B. OGDEN, EDWARD W. HUTCHINGS and
SAMUEL J. TILDEN, to me personally known to be the real persons described in, and who executed the foregoing instrument.
And the said WILLIAM B. OGDEN, being by me duly sworn,

said, that he resides in the City of Chicago and State of Illinois, and that he is the President of the Chicago and North Western Railway Company; that the seal affixed to the foregoing instrument is the common and corporate seal of said company, and was affixed thereto by their authority; and that he, as President, and EDWARD W. HUTCHINGS, as Treasurer, subscribed their names thereto, by the like authority; and that said EDWARD W. HUTCHINGS is the Treasurer of the said company. And said EDWARD W. HUTCHINGS acknowledged that he executed said instrument on behalf of, and as the act and deed of the said railway company, for the uses and purposes therein mentioned.

And the said SAMUEL J. TILDEN personally acknowledged that he executed the said instrument freely, and for the purpose therein stated. And I hereby certify that the said instrument is executed and acknowledged according to the laws of the State of New-York.

In testimony whereof, I have hereunto set my hand and affixed my seals of office, as such NOTARY and COMMISSIONER, at my office, in the City of New-York, the day and year first above written.

[L. S.]   [L. S.]   EDWIN F. COREY, JU'R.

(Form of Second Mortgage.)

THIS INDENTURE, made this first day of August, in the year of our Lord one thousand eight hundred and fifty-nine, between the CHICAGO AND NORTH WESTERN RAILWAY COMPANY, of the first part, and EDWARD W. HUTCHINGS, of the City of Boston, and State of Massachusetts, of the second part :
Whereas the said parties of the first part are a corporation, duly formed and organized in pursuance of a statute of the State of Wisconsin, entitled " An act to facilitate and authenticate the formation of a corporation, by the purchasers of the Chicago, St. Paul and Fond du Lac Rail-Road Company," approved March 14th, 1859, and of the laws of the State of Wisconsin ; and are likewise a corporation duly formed and organized in pursuance of a statute of the State of Illinois, entitled "An act to authorize the sale of the Chicago, St. Paul and Fond du Lac Rail-Road, and to enable the purchasers thereof to form a corporation," approved February 19th, 1859, and of the laws of the State of Illinois.

AND WHEREAS the said parties of the first part have become vested with the title to the rail-road formerly known as the Chicago, St. Paul and Fond du Lac Rail-Road, with its appurtenances, and of other property and franchises formerly owned or possessed by the Chicago, St. Paul and Fond du Lac Rail-Road Company, by deed bearing date the first day of July, one thousand eight hundred and fifty-nine, and made and delivered to the parties of the first part, by Samuel J. Tilden and Ossian D. Ashley, purchasers of the said rail-road property and franchises, in conformity to the aforesaid statutes and to the laws of the said States.

And whereas, for the purpose of funding debts which are liens upon certain of the aforesaid property, or have been assumed by the parties of the first part, as well as for the purpose of paying the consideration of the agreement between the said parties of the first part and the aforesaid purchasers, whereby the said railway and property were acquired, the said parties of the first part have resolved, in addition to the bonds issued and designated as first mortgage bonds, and secured by a trust deed to Samuel J. Tilden, trustee, and bearing date on the first day of July, 1859, to make and deliver a series of second mortgage bonds, to be secured by these presents, amounting in the aggregate to two millions of dollars, consisting of two thousand bonds, of one thousand dollars each; which said bonds are dated on the first day of July, one thousand eight hundred and fifty-nine; are payable on the first day of November, one thousand eight hundred and ninety, at the office or agency of the party of the first part in the City of New-York; bear interest from the first day of November, one thousand eight hundred and sixty, at the rate of six per centum per annum, payable semi-annually at the said office or agency, on the first days of May and November in each year; are equally secured by this instrument, and are in the form following:

No.   UNITED STATES OF AMERICA. $1,000.

STATES OF ILLINOIS AND WISCONSIN.

CHICAGO AND NORTH WESTERN RAILWAY COMPANY.

SECOND MORTGAGE BOND.

Know all men by these presents, that the Chicago and North Western Railway Company are indebted to E. W. Hutchings, of the City of Boston, or bearer, in the sum of one thousand dollars, lawful money of the United States of America, which the said Company promise and agree to pay to the said E. W. Hutchings, or bearer hereof, on the first day of November, A. D. one thousand eight hundred and ninety, at the office or agency of the said company in the City of New-York, with interest thereon from the first day of November, one thousand eight hundred and sixty, at the rate of six per centum per annum, payable semi-annually by the said company at their office or agency in the City of New-York, on the first days of May and November in each year, on the presentation and surrender of the annexed coupons as they severally become due. And in case of the non-payment of interest for any half year, if demanded, and the same remaining in arrear for six months thereafter, the principal shall become due and payable, as provided in the trust deed hereinafter mentioned.

This bond is one of a series of bonds of the same tenor, date and denomination, amounting in the aggregate to two millions of dollars, the payment of which is secured by a deed of trust, duly executed and delivered by the said railway company to E. W. Hutchings, trustee, and conveying the railway of the said company from Chicago to a point twenty miles northerly from Fond du Lac, and all the depot grounds, depots, equipments and other things pertaining thereto, and all the franchises of the said company, as by reference to the said trust deed, bearing date on the first day of August, A. D. 1859, and duly recorded, will more fully appear; subject, however, to the prior lien of a trust deed bearing date on the first day of July, 1859.

This bond entitles the person registered on the books of the company, as the holder thereof at the time of any general or special meeting of the stockholders, to one vote for every one hundred dollars of the par amount thereof, as a special stock created under the Act of the State of Wisconsin, approved March 14th, 1859, and the laws of that State and of Illinois, but such stock is not subject to assessment or entitled to dividends.

This bond shall not be valid or obligatory until it shall have been authenticated by a certificate endorsed hereon, and duly signed by the said trustee or his successor.

This bond may pass by delivery, or it may be registered on the books of the company at the option of any holder; and after such registration and the endorsement of a certificate thereof upon the bond, no transfer shall be valid unless such transfer be registered and endorsed as aforesaid, or unless the last registration be to bearer or in blank.

In witness whereof, the said company have caused their corporate seal to be hereto affixed, and their president and treasurer to sign, and their secretary to countersign the same, and have also caused the coupons hereto annexed to be signed by their assistant secretary, this first day of July, in the year of our Lord one thousand eight hundred and fifty-nine.

President.

Countersigned by

Treasurer.

Secretary.

All of which bonds, so issued or to be issued, are hereby declared and agreed to be given as consideration for the purchase of the said railway, property, rights and franchises, as hereinbefore recited.

NOW THIS INDENTURE witnesseth, that the parties of the first part, in consideration of the premises, and of one dollar to them in hand paid, the receipt whereof is here-

by acknowledged, and in order to secure the payment of the
principal and interest of the bonds aforesaid, issued or to be
issued as herein recited and provided, and every part of the
said principal and interest, as the same shall become payable,
according to the tenor of the said bonds, and of the coupons
thereto annexed, have granted, bargained, sold, conveyed and
transferred, and doth, by these presents, grant, bargain, sell,
convey and transfer unto the party of the second part, and
his heirs and assigns, and unto the successors of the said party
of the second part in the trust hereinafter created and set
forth, and the respective heirs and assigns of such successors,
all the railway of the parties of the first part, extending from
the City of Chicago, in the State of Illinois, to a point twenty
miles northerly from the City of Fond du Lac, and about
four miles northerly from the City of Oshkosh, in the State of
Wisconsin, by way of the Cities of Janesville, Fond du Lac
and Oshkosh, in the said State, and including that portion of
the said railway between the said cities of Janesville and the
La Crosse or Minnesota Junction, which is now in process of
construction, as the same shall be hereafter finished, as fully
and effectually as if the whole of the said railway were completed before the execution of these presents; including all
the railways, ways and rights of way, depot grounds and
other lands; all tracks, bridges, viaducts, culverts, fences
and other structures; all depots, station houses, engine houses,
car houses, freight houses, wood houses and other buildings;
and all machine shops and other shops; whether now held or
hereafter acquired for use, in connection with the said railway or the business thereof; and including, also, all locomotives, tenders, cars and other rolling stock or equipment, and
all machinery, tools, implements, fuel and materials for the
constructing, operating, repairing or replacing the said railway, or any part thereof, or any of its equipment or appurtenances, whether now held or hereafter acquired ; all of which
things are hereby declared to be appurtenances and fixtures of
the said railway ; and also all franchises connected with or relating to the said railway, or the construction, maintenance
or use thereof, now held or hereafter acquired by the said
parties of the first part; and all corporate and other franchises
which are now or may be hereafter possessed or exercised by
the said parties of the first part :

Together with all and singular the tenements, hereditaments and appurtenances thereunto belonging or in any wise
appertaining, and the reversions, remainders, tolls, incomes,
rents, issues and profits thereof; and also all the estate, right,

title, interest, property, possession, claim and demand whatsoever, as well in law as in equity, of the said parties of the first part, of, in and to the same, and any and every part thereof, with the appurtenances : *subject*, nevertheless, to all and singular the powers and authorities reserved or granted, in and by a certain indenture made and delivered by the parties of the first part to Samuel J. Tilden, trustee, and bearing date the first day of July, in the year one thousand eight hundred and fifty-nine, which said powers and authorities, and each of them, if and so often as exercised, shall operate to release from the lien of these presents, in the same cases, in the same manner, to the same extent, and with the same effect, as they shall operate to release from the lien of the aforesaid trust deed in which they are reserved, granted or declared, and to all the reservations, grants, conditions and provisions of the said indenture ; and subject to the prior lien of the said indenture upon all and singular the railway and its appurtenances, the property, rights, franchises and things of whatsoever name or nature, conveyed by these presents, or intended so to be; which said indenture was given to secure the payment of several series of bonds amounting in the aggregate to four millions and six hundred thousand dollars, with provision for the contingent issue of an additional amount not exceeding two hundred and fifty thousand dollars ; and also *subject*, nevertheless, in respect to certain of the aforesaid lands situate in the City of Chicago, and acquired for depot grounds, which are described in a trust deed of William B. Ogden to Azariah C. Flagg, bearing date the first day of January, one thousand eight hundred and fifty-seven, and recorded in the office of the Recorder of Cook County, in the State of Illinois, on the twenty-third day of February, one thousand eight hundred and fifty-seven, in book one hundred and twenty-one of deeds, page three hundred and sixty-four, and to the provisions of the said trust deed and the prior lien created thereby ; and in respect to certain other of the aforesaid lands, also situate and acquired as aforesaid, which are described in a trust deed of the said William B. Ogden to Richard H. Winslow, bearing date on the thirty-first day of May, one thousand eight hundred and fifty-eight, and recorded in the office of the said Recorder on the seventh day of August, one thousand eight hundred and fifty-eight, in book one hundred and fifty-six of deeds, page six hundred and twenty-five, and to the provisions of the said last mentioned trust deed, and the prior lien created thereby; the obligations secured by which said incumbrances, the parties of the first part have assumed and agreed to pay, and in evidence and security thereof, have executed and delivered a trust deed of the aforesaid lands to the said Azariah C. Flagg, bearing date the first day of July, one thousand eight hundred and fifty-nine, but to which, as respects the aforesaid lands, these presents are subject.

To have and to hold the above described premises and appurtenances, but subject to the reservations, conditions and provisions herein contained, unto the said party of the second part, and his heirs and assigns, and unto the several successors of the said party of the second part, in the trust hereby created, and their respective heirs and assigns, to the only proper use and behoof of the said party and his heirs and assigns, and of the said successors and their respective heirs and assigns, in trust, nevertheless, for the following purposes, to wit :

1. In case default shall be made by the parties of the first part, or their successors or assigns, in the payment of any interest on any of the aforesaid bonds according to the tenor of the coupons thereto annexed, or in the payment of any principal of any such bonds, as the same shall become demandable ; and if such default shall continue for the period of six months ; and if it shall be determined, in the manner hereinafter provided, that such default arose in whole or in part by reason of the omission or neglect to apply upon or towards the payment of the said interest the net earnings of the said railway, after paying the expenses of operating, repairing and replacing the said railway, and of conducting the business thereof, and paying all taxes, assessments, and all charges upon the same, or any part thereof, or upon any property embraced within these presents, so far as the same may be due, and making all payments, whether of interest or otherwise, which shall be due or demandable according to the provisions of the mortgage or trust deed hereinbefore mentioned, made by the said parties of the first part to Samuel J. Tilden, or due or demandable according to the provisions of the mortgage or trust deed hereinbefore mentioned, made by the said parties of the first part to Azariah C. Flagg ; or if instead of such determination in the manner hereinafter provided, a majority in amount of the holders for the time being of each class of the bonds secured by the said trust deed to the said Samuel J. Tilden shall consent, of which consent the certificate of the trustee or trustees for the time being under the said trust deed, and executed and acknowledged or proved in the manner required for the recording of

conveyances in the States of Illinois and Wisconsin, shall be conclusive evidence; provided, nevertheless, that neither such determination nor such consent shall be construed or shall avail in any manner to impair or affect the operation of the said trust deed to Samuel J. Tilden, or any powers or authorities or rights by virtue of the same, either of the trustee or any holder of any bonds secured thereby; then, and in either of such cases, it shall be lawful for the said trustee himself, or by his attorneys or agents, to enter into and upon all and singular the premises hereby conveyed, or intended so to be, and each and every part thereof; and himself, or by his attorneys or agents, to have, hold, use and enjoy the same; himself, or by his superintendents, managers, receivers or servants operating the said railway, and conducting the business thereof, and making, from time to time, all repairs and replacements, and all useful alterations, additions and improvements thereto, as fully as the parties of the first part might have done before such entry; and to collect and receive all tolls, freights, incomes, rents, issues and profits of the same, and of every part thereof; and after deducting the expenses of operating the said railway, and conducting its business, and of all the said repairs, replacements, alterations, additions and improvements, and all payments for taxes, assessments, charges or liens on the said premises, or any or every part thereof; and after paying all sums of money whether as interest or principal, or otherwise, which shall be or become due or demandable according to the provisions of the aforesaid trust deed, made by the parties of the first part to Samuel J. Tilden, in the manner and order therein provided, and all sums of money due or demandable according to the aforesaid trust deed made by the parties of the first part, to Azariah C. Flagg, in the manner and order therein provided, to apply the residue of the said net earnings to the payment of interest on the bonds secured by these presents, in the order in which such interest shall have become due or shall become due, and to the persons holding the coupons evidencing the right to such interest; and if the moneys applicable to such payments shall not suffice to make them in full, the said moneys shall be applied ratably towards such payment. And in case all the said payments shall have been made in full, and no sale shall have been made in conformity hereto, the said trustee shall restore the possession of the premises hereby conveyed unto the said party of the first part, its successors or assigns; provided, that if any of the defaults hereinbefore specified be subsequently made, such restoration shall not, nor shall any previous entry be construed to exhaust or in any manner impair the powers of entry or sale, or any powers hereby granted to or conferred upon the said trustee.

2. In case default shall be made as aforesaid, and shall continue as aforesaid, and in case the determination hereinbefore specified shall be made in the manner hereinafter provided, or the consent hereinbefore specified shall be given, it shall likewise be lawful for the said trustee, after entry as aforesaid, or other entry, or without entry, himself or by his attorneys or agents, to sell and dispose of all and singular the premises hereby conveyed, or intended so to be, or any portion thereof, and all right, benefit and equity of redemption of the parties of the first part, their successors and assigns, at public auction, in the City of New-York, or in the City of Chicago, or in such other place in the State of Wisconsin as the said trustee or his attorneys or agents may designate, or in any one or more of those places, and at such time or times as he or they may appoint, having first given notice of the place or places, and the time or times of such sale or sales, by advertisement published not less than three times a week, for eight weeks, in one or more newspapers in each of said cities of New-York and Chicago, or to adjourn the said sale or sales from time to time, in his or their discretion, and, if so adjourning, to make the same at the time or times, and place or places, to which the same may be so adjourned; and, as the attorney in fact of the said parties of the first part, their successors or assigns, for such purpose duly and irrevocably constituted, or in the name of the said trustee, to make and deliver to the purchaser or purchasers thereof, good and sufficient deed or deeds in the law for the same, in fee simple; which sale or sales, made as aforesaid, shall be a perpetual bar, both in law and equity, against the said parties of the first part, their successors and assigns, and all other persons claiming or to claim the said premises, or any part thereof, by, from or under them, or any of them; and, after deducting from the proceeds of such sale or sales, just allowances for all expenses of the said sale or sales, including attorneys' and counsel fees, and all other expenses, advances and liabilities which may have been made or incurred by the said trustee in the operating or maintaining the said railway, or managing of its business, and all payments for taxes, assessments, charges or liens on the said premises, or any part thereof, or in administering the said trust, as well as compensation for his own services, and paying the lien created by the aforesaid trust deed of said parties of the first part to the said Azariah O. Flagg, and

paying all sums of money, whether as interest, principal or otherwise, which shall be then due or demandable, according to the provisions of the aforesaid deed, made by the said parties of the first part to Samuel J. Tilden,—to apply the residue of such proceeds, after refunding, with interest at seven per cent., any advances to pay interest or principal of any lien prior to these presents, which may have been made or procured to be made in pursuance of any resolution or authority of holders of a majority in amount of the bonds hereby secured,—to the payment of the interest then due on the aforesaid bonds secured by these presents, in the order in which such interest shall have become due, and to the persons holding the coupons, evidencing the right to such interest, and next thereafter to the payment of the principal of the said last mentioned bonds; and in case the portion of the said proceeds which may be applicable, according to the aforesaid order of priority, to any of the aforesaid classes of payments, shall not suffice to make the payments of such class in full, the said portion shall be applied ratably towards the said payments.

And it is hereby declared, that the receipt or receipts of the said trustee shall be a sufficient discharge to the purchaser or purchasers of the premises, or any part thereof, for his or their purchase money; and that such purchaser or purchasers, his or their heirs, executors or administrators, shall not, after payment thereof, and having such receipt, be liable to see to its being applied upon or for the trusts and purposes of these presents, or in any manner howsoever, be answerable for any loss misapplication or non-application of such purchase money, or any part thereof, or be obliged to inquire into the necessity, expediency or authority of or for any such sale or sales.

Provided always, and the grant and conveyance herein contained are upon the express condition, that if the said parties of the first part shall well and truly pay, or cause to be paid, the interest on the said bonds, so issued or to be issued as aforesaid, as the same shall fall due and be demanded, and also the principal thereof, when the same shall fall due, or shall exhibit the said bonds, cancelled, to the said party of the second part, or his successor in the said trust, then the estate, title and interest of the party of the second part, and his successors in the trust, shall cease, determine and become void, but otherwise they shall remain in full force and virtue.

And the said parties of the first part hereby further covenant and agree to and with the said party of the second part, and his successors, that a book shall, at all times hereafter, be kept by the parties of the first part and their successors, at their office or agency in the City of New-York, which shall be designated as the Voting Register of the Second Mortgage Bondholders, and shall be distinct from the Transfer Register of the bonds ; that any holder of any of the said bonds shall be entitled to have his name and address, and the denomination of every of the said bonds held by him, entered in such registry on presenting, at the aforesaid office or agency, a written statement of the said particulars, signed by himself; and if required, duly verifying his title thereto by producing the bonds, or in such other mode as may be prescribed by the regulations for such verification ; that the parties of the first part may, in the first instance, prescribe the said regulations, subject to the power hereby declared of the said bondholders, acting by a majority in interest, to adopt, alter or repeal, from time to time, the said regulations, and generally to establish such as seem to them expedient; that such registration shall authenticate the right of the holder of every bond so registered to vote on the said bond, as provided therein, at every general and special meeting of the stockholders of the said parties of the first part; and shall also entitle the said holder to notice, in such mode and form as may be fixed by regulations prescribed or established as aforesaid, of all meetings of the second mortgage bondholders ; that the trustee for the time being shall at all times have free access to such book of registry, and shall, from time to time, and at all times, on his request in writing, be furnished with a copy thereof by the parties of the first part; but, nevertheless, shall have a right to require, at his option, that any act or resolution of the said bondholders affecting his duties or the interest of the trust hereby created, shall be authenticated by the signatures of all the persons assenting thereto, as well as by a minute of the proceedings of the meeting; that meetings of the second mortgage bondholders may be called by the trustee for the time being, or in such other mode as may be fixed by regulations prescribed or established as aforesaid, and the bondholders may vote thereat in person or by proxy ; and that such other regulations or by-laws, in respect to such meetings, may be from time to time made and established by the said bondholders, acting by a majority in interest, as to them shall seem expedient.

And the parties of the first part hereby covenant to, and with the party of the second part and his several successors in the trust hereby created, and his and their respective assigns, that the parties of the first part, and their successors and assigns, shall and will, from time to time, and at all times hereafter, execute, deliver and acknowledge all and every such further deeds, conveyances and assurances in the law for the better assuring unto the party of the second part, and his several successors in the trust hereby created, and his and their respective heirs and assigns, of the premises in manner as above conveyed or expressed, or intended to be conveyed, as well in reference to property or things at any time or times hereafter acquired, as to such as are now owned or possessed by the parties of the first part, or for the better effectuating of the intent and objects of these presents, as by the said party of the second part, or his several successors in the trust hereby created, or his or their respective assigns, or his or their counsel learned in the law, shall be reasonably advised, devised or required: And that the above described premises, and every part thereof, in the quiet and peaceable possession of the said party of the second part, and his several successors in the trust hereby created, and his and their respective heirs and assigns, against all and every person or persons lawfully claiming, or to claim the whole or any part thereof, the said parties of the first part shall and will warrant and forever defend.

It is mutually agreed, by and between the parties hereto, that in case of default as aforesaid it shall be the duty of the trustee for the time being to exercise the power of entry, or the power of sale hereby granted, or both, upon the requisition in writing of the holders of a majority in amount of the bonds secured by these presents; but holders of a majority in amount of such bonds at a meeting of the bondholders, duly held, or by an instrument in writing, signed by them, may instruct the said trustee to defer or omit the exercise of the said powers, or of either of them; and it is further agreed, as aforesaid, that the determination of the question, whether or not the aforesaid default shall have arisen by reason of the omission or neglect to apply the net earnings of the said railway, after paying the expenses and making the payments or prior lien hereinbefore fully specified and defined, to the payment of interest or principal of the bonds secured by these presents, shall be made in the following manner :

If the trustee under these presents, shall be of opinion that the default has arisen by reason of neglect or omission as aforesaid, or if he be requested in writing by holders of a majority in amount of the said bonds, he shall appoint one disinterested person, and the trustee under the first mortgage shall, within thirty days, after notice from the trustee under these presents, appoint another disinterested person, and the persons so first appointed shall select and appoint an umpire, and the three persons so appointed shall meet and hear, in a summary manner, the evidence upon the said question, until they, or a majority of them, are satisfied ; and shall decide the said question and also the amount of money so misapplied ; and the decision of the said persons, or of a majority of them, in writing, and acknowledged or proved in the manner requisite to entitle a conveyance to be recorded by the laws of the States of Illinois and Wisconsin, shall be a final and conclusive determination of the said question ; and if the trustee of the said first mortgage shall omit, for sixty days after such notification, to appoint such person, the trustee under these presents may make such appointment. *Provided*, nevertheless, and it is further agreed that, if, within six months after such determination, the parties of the first part or their successors shall pay to the trustee under these presents, the amount of moneys which shall, according to such determination, be so misapplied, the said trustee shall not exercise the powers of entry or sale hereby granted, or either of them.

And it is mutually agreed by and between the parties hereto, as a condition on which the party of the second part has assented to these presents, that until a default and requisition, as hereinbefore defined and provided, the trustee for the time being shall not be required to perform any active duty ; that the said trustee may at all times and in all cases act in the said trust by one or more of such attorneys, agents and servants as he may from time to time appoint or constitute, as validly and effectually in all respects as if acting personally ; that the said trustee shall not be, in any manner, responsible for any default or misconduct of any such attorney, agent or servant whom he may at any time so appoint or constitute, or for any thing other than his own wilful default or misconduct ; that the said trustee shall be entitled to just compensation for all services which he may hereafter render in his trust ; that a resolution adopted by a majority in interest of the said bondholders requesting, approving or ratifying any act or omission on the part of the said trustee shall be full and conclusive justification of him as against each and all of the holders of the bonds, and shall acquit and discharge him from all accountability to such holders for and in respect to such act or omission ; but this provision shall not be construed to authorize any deviation from the rule established by these presents for the distribution of net earnings or proceeds of the said railway and property among the bondholders; that the said trustee my resign and discharge himself of the trust created by these presents by notice in writing to the parties of the first part, or their successors or assigns, and also to the immediate successor of the said trustee, if such successor shall have been designated herein, or in conformity to the provisions herein contained; that the said trustee may be removed by the vote of a majority in interest of the holders of the aforesaid bonds; the said votes being had at meetings duly held of the said bondholders, and attested by an instrument under the hands and seals of the persons so voting, and acknowledged in the manner required in the States of Wisconsin and Illinois in order to entitle a conveyance to be recorded; that in case the party of the second part shall die, resign or be removed, his immediate successor shall be Ossian D. Ashley, of the city of New-York, and in case the said Ossian D. Ashley shall die, resign or be removed, or shall disclaim or decline to act, the second successor of the said trustee shall be Andrew H. Green, of the said city; that the trustee for the time being shall have power, with the consent of the holders of a majority in amount of the said bonds, to remove any immediate or other successor who may have been designated, and shall have power, with the like consent, to appoint an immediate or a second successor, in case either shall have died, resigned, or been removed, or shall have disclaimed or declined or become incapable or unfit to act; and shall have power, with the consent of holders of a majority in amount of the said bonds, to appoint, not exceeding two new trustees, to be associated with himself in the trust; that in case at any time hereafter any trustee shall die, or resign, or be removed, as herein provided, or by a court of competent jurisdiction, or in case any trustee shall become incapable or unfit to act in the said trust, and no successor shall have been provided in conformity hereto, a new trustee or new trustees, not exceeding three in number, may be appointed by the holders of a majority in amount of the said bonds; that the word trustee, as used in these presents, shall be construed to mean the trustee who may be at the time acting, or, if the number be increased, the trustees who may be at the time acting; that upon the accession or appointment of any new trustee or trustees, he or they shall become vested with all the powers and authorities and estates granted to or conferred upon the trustee or the party of the second part by these presents, and all the rights and interests requisite to enable the person or persons so acceding or appointed to execute the purposes of this trust, without any further assurance or conveyance; but all conveyances and other instruments shall be from. time to time executed by the said trustee, and by the parties of the first part, which the counsel of the said trustee shall reasonably devise or advise for the purpose of assuring the legal estate in the premises to the trustee or trustees, who shall for the time being be designated as successors in the said trust, or appointed as trustee or trustees; and upon the death, resignation or removal of any trustee, or an appointment in his place in pursuance of these presents, all his powers and authorities by virtue hereof shall cease; and if, and as soon as effectual provision shall have been made, for vesting the legal estate in the said premises in his successor or successors, all the estate, right, title and interest of the said trustee so dying, resigning or being removed, in the said premises, shall be divested and wholly cease and determine.

And it is hereby agreed between the parties to this indenture, that in the mean time, and until default shall be made in the payment of the interest or principal of the said bonds, or of some of them, or some part thereof, it shall be lawful for the said parties of the first part, and their successors, peaceably and quietly to have, hold, use, possess and enjoy the said premises, with the appurtenances, and to receive the incomes, tolls, rents, issues and profits thereof, to their own use and benefit, without any hindrance or interruption, suit or disturbance whatsoever, of or by the said party of the second part, or his successors in the trust, or any other person whatever lawfully claiming or to claim the same, by, from or under him or them or any of them.

In testimony whereof, the said parties of the first part have caused their corporate seal to be affixed to these presents, and the same to be attested by the signatures of their President and Secretary, and the said party of the second part has hereunto set his hand and seal, to testify his acceptance of the said trust, the day and year first above written.

[L. S.]   W. B. OGDEN, *President.*
       JAMES R. YOUNG, *Secretary.*
       E. W. HUTCHINGS, *Trustee.*   [L. S.]

Signed, sealed and delivered in the }
       presence of   }
       H. H. BOODY,
       EDWIN F. COREY, JUR.

UNITED STATES OF AMERICA,
STATE OF NEW-YORK, CITY AND COUNTY OF NEW-YORK, } *ss.*

Be it known, that on the eighth day of October, in the year one thousand eight hundred and fifty-nine, before me, the undersigned, Edwin F. Corey, Junior, resident in the City of New-York, and a commissioner, duly commissioned and qualified by the executive authority and under the laws of the State of Wisconsin, to take acknowledgment of deeds, &c., to be used or recorded therein, and a public notary in and for the State of New-York, by Letters Patent under the Great Seal of State, duly commissioned and sworn, personally appeared WILLIAM B. OGDEN, JAMES R. YOUNG and EDWARD W. HUTCHINGS, to me personally known to be the real persons described in, and who executed the foregoing instrument. And the said WILLIAM B. OGDEN, being by me duly sworn, said, that he resides in the City of Chicago and State of Illinois, and that he is the President of the Chicago and North Western Railway Company; that the seal affixed to the foregoing instrument is the common and corporate seal of said company, and was affixed thereto by their authority; and that he, as President, and JAMES R. YOUNG as Secretary, subscribed their names thereto, by the like authority; and that said JAMES R. YOUNG is the Secretary of the said company. And said JAMES R. YOUNG acknowledged that he executed said instrument on behalf of, and as the act and deed of the said railway company, for the uses and purposes therein mentioned.

And the said EDWARD W. HUTCHINGS personally acknowledged that he executed the said instrument freely, and for the purpose therein stated. And I hereby certify that the said instrument is executed and acknowledged according to the laws of the State of New-York.

In testimony whereof, I have hereunto set my hand and affixed my seals of office, as such NOTARY and COMMISSIONER, at my office, in the City of New-York, the day and year first above written.

[L. S.]   [L. S.]   EDWIN F. COREY, JUR.

www.ingramcontent.com/pod-product-compliance
Lightning Source LLC
Chambersburg PA
CBHW021415090426
42742CB00009B/1152